T0309871

Michael Marder

GRAFTS
WRITINGS ON PLANTS

Grafts
Writings on Plants
by Michael Marder

© Michael Marder
Published by Univocal

411 N. Washington Ave, Suite 10
Minneapolis, MN 55401

Designed & Printed by Jason Wagner

Distributed by the University of Minnesota Press

ISBN 9781937561673
Library of Congress Control Number 2016939295

TABLE OF CONTENTS

PART 3: *INTER*PRETATIONS

PART 4: *INTER*VIEWS

For Patrícia—
the grafts of the present
and those yet to come

GRAFTS
WRITINGS ON PLANTS

0. Grafting

Grafting: do we ever do anything other than that? And are we ever free from vegetal influences when we engage in its operations?

In agronomy, grafts are the shoots, or twigs, inserted into a slit of a tree. As soon as the sap of an insert mixes with that of the tree that receives it, the host is no longer the same as it was before. Either its flowers or fruits coexist with those of the grafted variety throughout the entire plant, or they change and acquire the characteristics of the graft, as in many species of apples. Grafting, therefore, foregrounds the plasticity and receptivity of vegetal life, its constitutive capacity for symbiosis and metamorphosis, its openness to the other at the expense of fixed identities (even the identity ensconced in genetics) revealed, by their very vitality, as illusory.

At the same time, grafts are not circumscribed to plants. They can also name a surgical procedure, whereby living tissue, most often skin, is transplanted from one part of the body to another, or from one body to another. When they are successful, that is to say, when the organism does not reject the tissues grafted onto it, these operations disclose the vegetal character of corporeality: of flesh proliferating on flesh, of skin breathing through its porous superficies like a leaf, of the entire body put together thanks to additions and superimpositions, not as a closed *either/or* totality but as a potential infinity of *and, and, and…* The very fact that grafts can refer to animal or human tissues as well as to plant parts testifies to the word's and the practice's quiet rebellion against the strictures of identity.

In an attempt to police category boundaries and to rectify the ensuing state of confusion, the English language also colors the semantics of the verb "to graft" with the sense of an inappropriate action, one that transposes X onto Y without regard for Y's specificities. (By way of illustration, the *Oxford*

Dictionary of Difficult Words cites incompatibilities between distinct political models: "Western-style government could not easily be *grafted onto* a profoundly different country."[1]) At best, such actions will result in the rejection of the graft by the host; at worst, they will be experienced as a suffocating imposition, lacking in respect to the local idiosyncrasies of that upon which they are grafted. What this meaning of grafting presupposes is that the introduction of the other overwrites the already existing biological, political, social, and other fabrics, occludes their native inscriptions, and violates the codes that govern their production. In short, it dismisses the possibility of a relation between two singularities, through which both are transformed beyond recognition and exceed the categories, systems of classification, or orders of being our thinking is accustomed to group them in.

Not coincidentally, I have just invoked writing and inscription in relation to grafts. Therein lies the word's etymological origin. Derived from the Greek verb *graphein*—"to write"—it predisposes us to view the relation between the host and the transplant in terms of the substratum for an inscription and that which is written on it. Ultimately, the difference between the writing and its support will disappear, but only on the condition that both would become different from what they used to be before grafting. True, letting go of past identity (or of the illusion that we had one) is far from painless; it requires an incision in the host and the separation of the graft from the initial context of its growth. In academic work, citations are the grafts *par excellence*; rather than weaving a seamless textile of words, we inevitably cut and paste, cite, plant, implant and transplant foreign texts onto the corpus we compose.

The physical cut that precedes grafting is anticipated in the Greek *graphion*, meaning "stylus" or "writing implement," made from the tapered tip of a scion. For a non-commercial exchange to happen between the two, the juices, sap, ink

1. "Graft," in *Oxford Dictionary of Difficult Words*, edited by Archie Hobson (Oxford: Oxford University Press, 2004), p. 196.

(blood?) need to flow in spots where a branch from another plant is thrust into the trunk and a stylus presses onto parchment, paper (skin?). Or, where the blood of friends, both of whom have prickled their fingers, mixes in an affirmation of a secret oath. Membranes, tissues, liquids, and surfaces must be exposed to one another in all their nudity for a graft to work, to exercise its transformative influence. But this exposure is, itself, something exceptionally difficult to achieve and to sustain, which is why it calls for procedures that appear to be violent. Only at the price of a prior, semi-forgotten violence can the sense of seamlessness and continuity be maintained.

* * *

Since my forays into a philosophy of the vegetal world in *Plant-Thinking*, I have been occupied (but also preoccupied, nearly obsessed) with the task of grafting human cognition and other processes onto their analogs in plants, and vice versa. As I explain in the introduction to that book, still without mentioning grafts, one of its main concerns is "how human thinking is, to some extent, de-humanized and rendered plant-like, altered by its encounter with the vegetal world."[2] That is to say: how is it possible for two kinds of thinking to blossom or come to fruition together, on the same trunk/body/corpus.

Besides human thought and plant-thinking, art and philosophy, the sciences and the humanities, as well as intellectual and personal histories have all been grafted onto one another in subsequent articles and books, such as *The Philosopher's Plant* and *Through Vegetal Being*.[3] For all their multifaceted, interdisciplinary nature, the theoretical studies of and practical engagements with plants have had one thing in common: they have thrived at the edges, neither fully inside nor outside different methodologies, approaches, points of view, and

2. Michael Marder, *Plant-Thinking: A Philosophy of Vegetal Life* (New York: Columbia University Press, 2013), p. 10.

3. Michael Marder, *The Philosopher's Plant: An Intellectual Herbarium* (New York: Columbia University Press, 2014); Luce Irigaray & Michael Marder, *Through Vegetal Being* (New York: Columbia University Press, 2016).

people. In other words, they have shared the characteristic of being grafts.

Grafts unfolds (and grafts unfold) within the in-between space where previously unimagined forms of thinking eventually come to life. Moving across disciplinary lines, I combine the insights of plant science with the history of philosophy, semiotics, literary compositions, and political theory. Co-authoring some of the texts with other philosophers, plant scientists and artists, I allow their insights to be grafted onto mine, and mine onto theirs. Weighing in on contemporary debates regarding the ethics of biotechnology, dietary practices, or political organization, I insert an unmistakable vegetal perspective into bodies of work, in which it is foreign. Transferring the living tissue of my own texts into another context, I help them live better and more fully than they would otherwise.

In the spirit of exploring the intermediacy broached by grafts, the book is divided into four parts, each of them focusing on a particular in-between, signaled by the Latin prefix *inter*:

1. *Inter*ventions
2. *Inter*actions
3. *Inter*pretations
4. *Inter*views

Part 1 is comprised of my theoretical contributions to themes in plants and philosophy, politics, ethics, and the scientific method.

Part 2 features texts I co-authored with colleagues in philosophy and plant sciences, including Monica Gagliano, Yogi Hendlin, František Baluška, and Luis Garagalza.

Part 3 consists of my interpretations of the role of plants in the writings of philosophers, theorists, and literary authors such as Friedrich Nietzsche, Jean-Jacques Rousseau, Henry Thoreau, Clarice Lispector, Gilles Deleuze, Georges Bataille, and others.

Part 4 gathers my interviews on plants, granted to Joe Humphreys (*The Irish Times*), Margarida Mendes, Ilda Teresa Castro, Heidi Norton & Monica Westin (*BOMB Magazine*), along with my debate with Prof. Gary Francione. In many cases, only abbreviated versions of these discussions have been previously published, which means that they will be appearing here in their entirety for the first time.

PART 1: *INTER*VENTIONS

1. For the love of plants

Most people believe that I am elaborating a philosophy of vegetal life out of an intense love of plants. Some time ago, I co-authored with Patrícia Vieira an article titled "Writing Phytophilia: Philosophers and Poets as Lovers of Plants."[4] In that text I did not address the question of my personal motivation, choosing to focus, instead, on the curious case of Jean-Jacques Rousseau. The most diligent of readers are advised to glean some of the answers from the already mentioned quasi-autobiographical book, *Through Vegetal Being*, which I wrote with Luce Irigaray. For now, I would like to register in writing my amazement with the nearly automatic association between the topic one thinks through–however passionately–and the feeling of love. Do we necessarily fall in love with the objects of our inquiries? Is it thanks to this affect that what we think about can turn the tables and start interrogating *us*?

The very word *philosophy*, as is well known, alludes to love (*philia*) directed toward wisdom (*sophia*). Note that the philosopher's love is not a particular attachment to this or that thing, but to all of wisdom (Heidegger used to say "to being as such and as a whole"). This strange affection is supposed to be just because it does not privilege a single being at the expense, and to the exclusion, of all the others. Now, the affection for plants is not universal, unlike wisdom or being, and therefore the love showered upon them would be a deprivation in relation to other elements of the environment, notably animals. That, at least, has been the gist of certain criticisms I have received on the heels of my efforts to develop an ethics of vegetal life.

I will return to the issue of universality and exclusion in just a moment. A prior question is one I have already

4. Patrícia Vieira & Michael Marder, "Writing Phytophilia: Philosophers and Poets as Lovers of Plants," *Frame: A Journal of Literary Studies*, 26(2), November 2013, pp. 39-55.

formulated: Is it inevitable that we love whatever we think about or "work" on? The case of John Maynard Keynes comes to mind in this regard. One of the twentieth century's most important economists, he was an aesthete, a literature and fine arts aficionado who deemed purely economic pursuits ignoble. It is also hard to believe that Holocaust historians adulate the subject of their investigations or that cancer researchers adore the disease that they study. This would suggest that, often, what draws our scholarly attention are the "sore spots," that is to say, troublesome topics and traumatic concerns, which neither leave us unmoved nor spark the flame of love. If they verge on an obsession, these sensitive areas may not just draw us toward themselves but devour us, a bit like a cosmic black hole. In them, through them, we are claimed by the essential—by the demand for justice. Hence, one would not need to experience "green love" (or to turn into a "tree hugger," though there is nothing wrong with that) to be attracted to a way of thinking about and with vegetation. To become preoccupied with plants, it would be sufficient to heed the call of justice that has not yet been rendered.

We ought to broaden our conception of love from the financially inflected "affective investment" into something or someone to a striving, an attraction, at once physical and psychic. In ancient and medieval thought, love was not really (at any rate, not primarily) an emotion; it was a force that compelled a stone to move toward the earth, a plant to sunlight, or a human soul to the Good.

Refreshingly, the evacuation of the emotional component from love brings this phenomenon closer to plants. It follows, in fact, that plants are the most loving of existents, in that they strive everywhere: toward sunlight as well as toward moisture, toward the dark of the earth and toward swift airflows. The universal striving of philosophy to being "as such and as a whole" (without exception; without any detail reckoned uninteresting) is an idealized replay of vegetal love in all its physicality. So what if, in our attraction to plants, we do not confine ourselves to one type of being but, on the contrary, extend ourselves to countless organic and inorganic worlds through the elemental intersection where they grow? What if a plant is as close as one can get to something like the singular universality of life or of nature?

Elsewhere, I've written a thing or two on vegetal love. I have, nevertheless, neglected to take my observations to a very simple conclusion: Plants expose themselves to the outside, and their exposure is erotic well before the evolution of flowers with their unique version of sexuality. The contiguity they establish with the soil, moisture, and solar energy is their mode of a caress—an elemental caress at that. Is there anything more erotic than being-in-the-world as handing the body (vegetal, animal, human) over to exteriority?

I know that this suggestion sounds provocative. But it is a necessary counterweight to the image of plants as colonizers, conquering space and spreading their "selfish genes" over it. The same event of an exuberant vegetal proliferation may be interpreted in two (or more) drastically dissimilar ways: as an aggressive act of conquest or as an act of love, of an immense and virtually limitless attraction to the outside. Both of these hermeneutical options are symptomatic of the human projection onto plants, implicitly treated as screens for our self-image. Colonizers are more likely to see estranged replicas of themselves in the foreign green environs, while those open to the world are prone to perceiving such openness in others (not only in human others). A little exaggeration of the loving component in plant behavior will do no harm in light of the long history of their demonization: the Amazon, for instance, was described as a "green desert" under the Brazilian dictatorship, and the jungle was portrayed as a "green hell" in James Whale's eponymous film from 1940.

That said, not everything depends on the frame of mind in which we find ourselves. Plants are not blank surfaces for the figuration of our fantasies. They have their own preferences for specific neighboring species; attract particular insects; and favor sunnier or shadier spots, in keeping with their variety.

Their attraction to exteriority is not made of one cloth, expressing as it does precise choices grounded in evolutionary adaptive decisions. Love is discrimination, even when its effects are universal.

On the whole, is philosophy's love of being as such also attracted to non-being, to pure nothingness? Does the love of wisdom incorporate stupidity, which is not the same as not-knowing, as Socrates never tired of professing? Attraction unfolds within certain limits; otherwise, love's tending toward… would be gradually distended until it flipped into its opposite, indifference. A commitment to universality does not mean thinking and loving all that is in equal measure or on an equal footing. The only viable way toward the universal passes through a singularity. For me, plants are these "singular universals," wholes in parts and parts in wholes. In a word, de-limitations. Loving them, we love the love of all that is.

2. Vegetal friendship

Let's begin with the common understanding of friendship. We call "friends" those of our peers who have interests and hobbies akin to ours, with whom we spend a portion of our spare time, attend cultural and social events, share a laugh or a moment of sadness. We can sneer, as Aristotle does in his *Nicomachean Ethics*, at the instrumental motivations of people who initiate friendships as a means to some external end and brag that they've "got friends in high places." Even more so today, the prevalent practice of networking tinges all social interactions with utility-maximizing objectives. One thing is nonetheless clear: a friend is someone who stands out from the undifferentiated mass of humanity (as well as from the semi-undifferentiated background of a social network), is individuated, and, in important respects, considered to be similar to ourselves. And what about the vast majority of people who are not our friends? Modern liberalism teaches us to treat them with universal apathy and neutrality, so long as they are not perceived as a threat; other worldviews may deem whoever is not presently a friend to be a potential friend or, conversely, an enemy.

Taking as an axiom the assertion that friendship hinges on similarity, the more we identify with a creature, the greater the likelihood that we would befriend it. A non-human animal can be a friend, or a companion, provided that we recognize and respond to each other's emotions, share time together (for instance, walking in a park), and so forth. The freedom and reciprocity of the animal's response is somewhat dubious, and such doubts are significant, assuming that friendship is a freely chosen arrangement, as the very English word *friend* intimates through its association with *free* (both derive from the proto-Indo-European root *pri-*, "to love"). Wild, undomesticated, and therefore freer animals spend but a fleeting moment with us, mostly gazing with curiosity, assessing whether we are threatening, a potential source of food, or simply irrelevant. When unprovoked, they tend to

27

turn their backs and treat us as good old liberals do, leading us to the deduction that they do not wish to be our friends. But then, again, there is no freedom in instrumentally acquired human friendships, where necessity dictates the terms of a relationship, either. Is it so preposterous to think that the friends we use as means to a goal are our pets, or that we are theirs, depending on the way the imbalance of power plays itself out?

More interesting though is the question of whether a plant or a god could be a friend. Can we have friends in places so low that they partly dwell in the soil? Or so high—higher than high—that their abode is above this world? Such a possibility seems to undermine what we took to be the basis of friendship, namely similarity in a way of acting or living that permits friends to share their interests and time. How does one spend time with an eternal, atemporal being, like (a) god? Or with a creature whose time-scale and response is drastically different from and typically much slower than that of human consciousness?

Imagine that you sit for hours on end under a tree you like (say, an olive tree). In doing so, you do not necessarily participate in the temporality of that tree, unless, through a deliberately honed practice of meditation, you alter your own consciousness, your own perception of time and slow it down enough to approximate that of the plant you are with. Be this as it may, friendship demands a minimum of synchronicity among friends who are "on the same page" if not in terms of their interests, then at least in terms of the structure of their experience of time and place. Formulated otherwise, friendship is willingness to share a world (which is not the same thing as the environment or the universe) across unavoidable differences in perspective between the I and the other.

Despite some promising leads, we would hit an impasse, insofar as the thinking of vegetal friendship (and friendship as such) is concerned, should we continue treating the parties to this relation as monolithic. It is advisable to consult a lineage that extends from Sigmund Freud to Carl Schmitt and Jacques Derrida, all of whom, in one way or another, expose the myth of the subject's inner psychic unity. Before addressing the issues involved in associations with external others, we should ask: Am I necessarily my own friend? Could I be an enemy to myself, harming or undercutting myself, if only unconsciously?

All of us, after all, live out of sync with ourselves, desperately trying to create synergies between the time of the unconscious and the traditional phenomenological flux of time-consciousness. At the extreme, when we grow oblivious to ourselves or become our own worst enemies, we may lapse into a schizophrenic state that merely exacerbates these preexisting mental fissures and gaps. Seeing that things are so complex at the level of my own self-identification, to discover similarities with the other is to foreground a portion of our psychic life, of which we (and the other) approve. Internal and external asynchoricity remains in effect, these fragile bridges notwithstanding.

In plants, the distinction between self and other, presupposed in any contemplation of friendship, is still thornier than in human subjectivity. Scientists (e.g., UC Davis's Richard Karban) study what they call "kin recognition" in plants—a biochemical detection and interpretation of certain specimens as "the same" and "the other." Depending on the identity of their neighbors, the behavior of plants changes: the roots are more extensive and dense in proximity to "strangers" than to "relatives." While kin recognition primarily deals with something like family ties, there are also instances of compatibility or incompatibility between various species. Every gardener knows that some seedlings should never be planted next to each other (for instance, peas and fennel), whereas others are "companion plants" (for example, tomato and calendula, which actually repels tomato worms). It is also a matter of broad consensus that plants are very good at creating alliances with particular insects, whom they summon to spread their pollen (bees, butterflies, etc.) or to repel attacking herbivores. As Consuelo de Moraes, Mark Mescher, and James Tumlinson note in *Nature*: "Plants respond to insect herbivory by synthesizing and releasing complex blends of volatile compounds, which provide important host-location cues for insects that are natural enemies of herbivores."[5]

In light of this multifaceted evidence, the conclusion that plants too have their friends and enemies, labeled without further ado "natural," is appealing. But a nagging suspicion lingers on: Aren't the scientists, too, projecting human group-ings onto the plant world? This is not to say that friendship and enmity are wholly inapplicable to the flora; what I mean, rather, is that we will not advance one iota in establishing how these concepts apply to other living beings, unless we account for their subjectivities.

I've already said that the topic of subjectivity is even thornier in plants than in humans, because the boundaries between the vegetal self and its other are incredibly porous. If a human subject is legion, then its vegetal counterpart is a legion of le-gions, comprised of self-replicating parts that can often sub-sist outside the provisional whole they comprise. Sometimes, various vegetal parts can be relatively unconcerned with one another. At other times, a hermaphroditic plant may activate the genetic mechanisms of "self-incompatibility" (SI) that block self-pollination. Most often, however, vegetal parts are highly sociable and symbiotic, participating on the same lev-el, as nearly autonomous friends, in a community that makes up a plant or in plant communities that add up to a still great-er botanical society. *Mutatis mutandis*, in vegetal friendship, the multiplicity that I (psychically, spiritually, physically) am reaches out to the multiplicity that a plant is—a situation that is not all that different from friendship between two or more human beings. Given the complexities of my own friendship or enmity with myself, redoubled by analogous intricacies in the constitution of my friend, there will always be coun-terforces that pull us apart, away from each other and from

---

5. Consuelo de Moraes, Mark Mescher, & James Tumlinson, "Caterpillar-in-duced nocturnal plant volatiles repel conspecific females", *Nature*, 410, March 2001, pp. 577-580.

ourselves, that is to say, from the predominant tendency of the innumerable forces that make us up.

My friend, Brianne Donaldson, suggests that "vegetal friendship" can refer at the same time to friendship with vegetation and friendship marked by vegetal qualities. The inherent ambiguity of the expression she points out is extremely helpful: as soon as we contemplate the scenario of a friendship with plants, we are reminded that all friendships are vegetal, no matter who they are forged with, to the extent that they involve a resonance of multiplicities comprising the subjectivities of friends. Cicero had a premonition of this difficulty, writing in his treatise on friendship: "For the essence of friendship being that two minds become as one, how can that ever take place if the mind of each of the separate parties to it is not single and uniform, but variable, changeable, and complex?"[6] Or, to reformulate in our terms: What is similitude between two, neither of whom is the same as her- or himself? How can friends grow together, if each undergoes metamorphoses and grows, plant-like, never being the same as before? Their growing-with, in the absence of a guaranteed common ground, is a promising avenue for thinking about and practicing vegetal friendship.

---

6. Cicero, *Two Essays: On Old Age and on Friendship* (London & New York: Macmillan, 1903), p. 199.

3. Smart as an oak?

There is a long-standing bias that considers human beings as the sole intelligent creatures on earth. If intelligence is defined on the basis of our behavioral traits, including the capacities to speak or to think with the help of abstract concepts, then a self-fulfilling prophecy of human exceptionalism is unavoidable. Starting from ourselves (but who is "ourselves"? is not *the human* always culturally specific as well as gender specific?), using ourselves as the yardstick for everything that matters, we only find what we have hidden at the outset of this treasure hunt, its outcome predetermined before it has had a chance to begin. *Homo sapiens* appears to be the exclusive seat of *sapiencia* (Latin for *wisdom*) factored into the very name of our species.

For scientists, however, the superiority of human intelligence over other primates is a mere hypothesis to be tested and subsequently verified or declined. That is what Esther Herrmann, of the Max Planck Institute for Evolutionary Anthropology in Leipzig, and her associates set out to do by evaluating and comparing the "general reasoning" and "social-cognitive skills" of humans, chimpanzees and orangutans. Their conclusions, published in the journal *Science*, might come as a shock. Chimps and young children showed remarkably similar results on certain measures of the IQ (Intelligence Quotient) tests including spatial and quantitative abilities. Yet, both orangutans and chimps underperformed, in comparison to humans, on skills related to "dealing with the social world."[7]

Much depends, of course, on how we construe social skill and what we count as such: learning from others, cooperation in problem solving, or other phenomena. What is crucial, in my view, is that humans are not superior to certain non-human

7. Esther Herrmann, et al. "Humans Have Evolved Specialized Skills of Social Cognition: The Cultural Intelligence Hypothesis", *Science*, vol. 317, no. 5843, pp. 1360-1366. DOI: 10.1126/science.1146282.

animals *even within the confines of a truly anthropocentric concept of general reasoning*. Cultural and scientific grounds are therefore quite ready for a cross-species conception of intelligence and its corresponding measurement in redesigned IQ tests.

Whether acknowledged or not, the real bone of contention is the meaning of intelligence, and that is where philosophers can join the conversation that has already drawn evolutionary biologists, anthropologists, and cognitive scientists into its midst. If we attempt to adopt the standpoint of the universal, well in excess of the limited context and realities of *Homo sapiens*, we will quickly realize that what we call *intelligence* is a feature of life itself, or, more precisely, of the multifaceted exchanges between an organism and its environment.

So vital are these interactions that authors of the likes of Aldo Leopold and Gregory Bateson insist on making the relational whole *organism-environment* the basic unit of intelligence. Now, a drastic revamping of the concept of intelligence along the lines Leopold and Bateson suggest would prompt us to admit under its heading not only non-human primates but also other animals, plants, fungi, and unicellular organisms.

In my *Plant-Thinking*, I accentuated some formal similarities among the mechanisms plants, animals, and humans use in their interaction with the environment. As I wrote in that text: "The sensitivity of the roots seeking moisture in the dark of the soil, the antennae of a snail probing the way ahead, and human ideas or representation we project, casting them in front of ourselves, are not as dissimilar to one another as we tend to think."[8] Within the scheme of survival, each of these "devices" functions as a means to an end, toward procuring the resources necessary for life from the outside world and avoiding (or protecting an organism from) the dangers that lurk there.

8. Marder, *Plant-Thinking*, p. 27.

Perhaps we could argue that the exceptional character of human intelligence lies in the possibility of asking *why?* and *what for?* rather than *how?* But the questions and thinking of ends, glorified in ancient Greek philosophy, are particularly out of fashion today, in an age enamored with the values of efficiency and productivity. If it takes place at all, the contemplation of reasons for something—why it is the way it is—happens not when things work smoothly but, on the contrary, when a malfunction creeps into the means we are accustomed to using in order to achieve our unexamined goals. The supposed marker of human exceptionalism is thus a sure symptom of non-adaptation, the incongruity between us and our milieu, an incompatibility between the environment and ourselves.

The paradox of our intelligence is sharply outlined here. One of the most successful species on the planet, spread over the entire surface of the earth, *Homo sapiens* threatens to destroy its own and other species' life-support systems. Our evolutionary success is a spectacular failure; our marvelous capacity for adaptation that molds any environment to our needs is, simultaneously, a catastrophic non-adaptation to the finite and fragile ecosystems we strive to dominate and control. How to measure this strange intelligence that is indistinguishable from stupidity? With the help of what IQ tests?

Seeking examples of intelligence in extra-terrestrial worlds or in humanly devised artificial systems is another marker of smart stupidity, which overlooks the wisdom embodied in non-human forms of life. In order to reverse millennia of disregard in the West, nothing short of devising a cross-species and cross-kingdoms measure of intelligence would do—call it a *general biological Intelligence Quotient* (in short: gb-IQ)—that would assess how successfully participants as diverse as an oak, a mouse, and a human adapt to their respective environments, collaborate with others, solve problems, and so forth.

We would not be able to administer a questionnaire to an oak or to a mouse, but neither is it possible to do so with a three-year-old child. Our interpretative faculties would have to work hard if we are to carry out a gb-IQ exercise. Furthermore, problem solving, collaboration, and adaptation would need to be indexed to the appropriate environments and requirements of each kind of organism, be it an underground labyrinth of mineral resources and moisture in the case of a tree or a complex network of social interactions holding the promise of positive reinforcement in the case of a human child. Although many of the circumstances are going to be wildly dissimilar, a common ground will gradually emerge (admittedly, thanks to our power of generalization and abstraction) for a less species-biased conception of intelligence.

Let's say that a gb-IQ test could be administered, with the myriad of imperfections that are bound to plague this project. Then, researchers are likely to discover areas of overlap between, as well as variations within, each participating species. Not all oaks will be equally smart, nor all mice uniformly intelligent, nor all humans the same when it comes to their IQ. Conceivably, there will even be some oaks smarter than some mice, or certain mice smarter than certain humans. The acceptance of this outcome would be a sign of humility and of intelligence on our part.

4. Plant-thinking is not species-thought

When our considerations of living beings rely on the language of *species*, they imperceptibly slip back into the jargon of early Scholasticism. It is unclear to me why the scientific methods of studying diverse forms of life have to stay frozen in that exact moment of European thought. They neither recall the Greek beginnings of the "systematic" investigations of nature nor catch up with the more recent developments in, say, quantum physics (or, closer to home, evolutionary theory). The outdated method of classifying plants, animals, fungi, etc. has a profound impact on our mode of seeing and treating them, which means that a change in how we order living beings would go a long way toward transforming our ontological and ethical relations to them.

The writings of "the last Roman and the first Scholastic," Boethius, are especially pertinent to what I refer to as "species-thought." Through induction from "singular things," Boethius claims, it is possible to arrive at their likeness (*similitudo*), which is the foundation for the concept of species: "…a species should be considered as nothing other than a thought (*cogitatio*) collected from the substantial likeness of many individuals which differ by number, whilst a genus is a thought collected from the likeness of species" (*2InIsag.* 166:16-18). From the standpoint of an already formed species-thought, however, the differences among the individuals that comprise it are accidental and superficial, in the same way that from the perspective of the genus the distinctions among the species are inessential. To continue working with the notions of species, genera, and kingdoms (note how the latter superimpose a monarchical structure on modes of living) is to capitulate before the power of abstraction, oblivious to singularity. Even if we stress the multiplicity of such categories, they will remain shackled to the actual or potential unity of a higher-level universal. It is as though we first placed living beings in hermetically sealed boxes, and then tried to air these containers by carving out windows, through which they could communicate with each other and with the world.

In broad brushstrokes, the heavy Scholastic heritage is the background for the reception of the philosophies of plant and animal life developed today. I am often asked, tongue-in-cheek: "You concentrate on plants. But what about fungi-thinking? Or algae-thinking? Or even mineral-thinking? Why exclude these other categories of organic and inorganic entities?" These questions are misguided, because they presume that I subscribe to the Scholastic division of the world into species, genera, and so forth.

Actually, "plant-thinking" has little in common with "species-thought." Although it might seem that I privilege the biological Kingdom *Plantae*, I do not intend it as a reference to some generic, abstract, nonexistent being that would encompass tulips, sequoias, and moss. Rather, "plants" stand for a tendency of living and thinking that promotes growth, decay and metamorphosis. This vital tendency, vector, or trajectory cuts across Boethius's "substantial likeness" and difference among individuals; it pertains to various kingdoms, classes, orders, families, and so on. That is why there is nothing odd in recognizing and cultivating "the plant in us," which is to say, the vegetal trajectory that certain aspects of our lives follow. And that is also why I can maintain that plants are radically other, to the extent that our habitual ways of being in the world and vectors of living diverge in some respects (e.g., humans are not sessile beings, with all the implications of this for our uprooted growth).

Attentive readers will observe that I emphasize thinking, and not thought, because my point of departure is not the substantial similitude of comparable objects but the differentials, at times approaching zero, between living vectors, including those moving "inside" ourselves. The frozen molds of thought correspond to the static realities they capture, determine, and define, separating these realities from all the others with the help of something like conceptual walls. Conversely, thinking befits the dynamic ontological tracks that have been contained within the limits of categories for too long, above all, those of species and genera. Perhaps, "befits" is not the right word here, since the living vectors I have invoked are, *at one and the same time*, the trajectories of material, spatialized, extended, constantly metamorphosing thinking. Ironically, I may end up re-confirming the insight of Parmenides, who is usually associated with a static and inflexible ontology, that it is the same thing to be and to think. Indeed, outside the horizons of species-thought, there is no difference between "plant" (being) and "thinking": in their life processes, the plants themselves think, strive or tend toward…, while thinking plants, grows, changes, decays.

For all the innovations of his process philosophy, Alfred North Whitehead was wrong to ascribe, in retrospect, Scholastic categories to Aristotle: "Aristotle's science of classification into genera, and species, and sub-species is the science of mutually exclusive classification. It develops Plato's suggestion of a science of 'Division.'"[9] Greek classifications were, precisely, not mutually exclusive, to the extent that, failing to live up to their end or *telos*, certain "higher" beings could become quite indistinguishable from the "lower" ones. This is what happens in Aristotle's *Metaphysics*, according to which, if humans disobey the precepts of formal logic—notably, the principle of non-contradiction—they become plant-like. Against relativism *avant la lettre*, Aristotle writes: "If, however, all men alike are both right and wrong, no one can say anything meaningful; for one must then at the same time say these and also other things. And he who means nothing, but equally thinks and does not think, in what respect does his condition differ from that of a plant?" (1008b). Negatively and with disdain, then, he outlines plant-thinking in the converging trajectories of the human and the plant outside formal-logical parameters. There is nothing mutually exclusive about the layers of vitality Aristotle calls *psukhē* ("soul") predicated upon one another; as I note in my *The*

9. Alfred North Whitehead, *Adventures of Ideas* (New York: The Free Press, 1933), pp. 137-8.

Philosopher's Plant, *psukhē*'s vegetal configuration "traverses biological kingdoms and species."[10] Strip the human stratum of "rational thought" and you will discover a humanoid plant, someone who or that, equally thinking and not thinking, merely vegetates—he implies with some irony. In my view, this is the groundwork of plant-thinking, which has little to do with the logic of species and kingdoms.

From there, the alternative to species-thought winds through Plotinus's "growth-thought," Avicenna's love, Spinoza's modes, Leibniz's expression, Schelling's "minimal irritability," Bergson's torpor with the possibility of sudden awakening… But it is always to plants that this other thinking returns, drawing inspiration from their proliferation that disregards all barriers (whether made of actual concrete or of concepts) and that even transcends the opposition between total immanence and pure transcendence. Like a living, growing plant, human thinking hardens on the outside and draws support from the exoskeleton-like solidness of its trunk or bark, which is actually the byproduct of its life-process. Only when reduced *in toto* to the already lifeless exterior layer, does it fit within the determinate outlines of thought. Faced with this situation, it is a grave error to chop down the plant of our thinking-thought; instead, we should peel its outer crusts so as to let the sap flow once again.

10. Michael Marder, *The Philosopher's Plant: An Intellectual Herbarium* (Columbia University Press, 2014), p. 31.

5. Ethics and a pea
(or, if peas can talk, should we eat them?)

Imagine a being capable of processing, remembering, and sharing information—a being with potentialities proper to it and a world of its own. Given this brief description, most of us will think of a human person, some will associate it with an animal, and virtually no one's imagination will conjure up a plant.

Since November 2, 2011, however, one possible answer to the riddle is *Pisum sativum*, a species colloquially known as the common pea.[11] On that day, a team of scientists from the Blaustein Institute for Desert Research published the results of their research, revealing that a pea plant subjected to drought conditions communicated its abiotic stress to other such plants, with which it shared its rooting volumes. Through the roots, it relayed to its neighbors the biochemical message about the onset of drought, prompting them to react as though they, too, were in a similar predicament.

Curiously, having received the signal, plants not directly affected by this particular environmental stress factor were better able to withstand adverse conditions when these actually occurred. This means that the recipients of biochemical communication could draw on their "memories"—information stored at the cellular level—to activate appropriate defenses and adaptive responses when the need arose.

In 1973, the publication of *The Secret Life of Plants*, by Peter Tompkins and Christopher Bird, which portrayed vegetal life as exquisitely sensitive, responsive and in some respects comparable to human life, was generally regarded as pseudoscience. Granted: the authors were not scientists, and the results reported in that book, many of them outlandish, could not be reproduced. But today, new, hard scientific data appears

---

11. Omer Falik, et al., "Rumor Has It...: Relay Communication of Stress Cues in Plants." *PLoS One*, Vol. 6, No. 11, November 2011, pp. 1-6.

to be buttressing the book's fundamental idea that plants are much more complex than previously thought.

The research findings of Omer Falik and his team form yet another building block in the growing fields of plant intelligence studies and neurobotany that, at the very least, ought to prompt us to rethink our relation to plants. Is it morally permissible to submit to total instrumentalization living beings that, albeit lacking a central nervous system, are capable of basic learning and communication? Should their swift response to stress leave us unaffected, while animal suffering provokes intense feelings of pity and compassion?

Evidently, empathy might not be the most appropriate ground for an ethics of vegetal life. But novel indications concerning the responsiveness of plants, their interactions with the environment and with each other, are sufficient to undermine all simple, axiomatic solutions to eating in good conscience. When it comes to a plant, it turns out to be not only a *what* but also a *who*, an agent in its milieu, with its own intrinsic value or version of the good. Inquiring into justifications for consuming vegetal beings thus re-conceived, we reach one of the final frontiers of dietary ethics.

Recent findings in cellular and molecular botany mean that eating preferences, too, must practically distinguish vegetal what-ness from who-ness, while striving to keep the latter intact. The work of such discernment is incredibly difficult because the subjectivity of plants is not centered in a single organ or function but is dispersed throughout their bodies, from the roots to the leaves and shoots. Nevertheless, this dispersion of vitality holds out a promise of its own: the plasticity of plants and their wondrous capacity for regeneration, their growth by increments, quantitative additions, or reiterations of already existing parts does little to change the form of living beings that are neither parts nor wholes because they are not hierarchically structured organisms. The "renewable" aspects of perennial plants may be accepted by humans as a gift of vegetal being and integrated into their diets.

It would be harder to justify the cultivation of peas and other annual plants that humans devote in their entirety to externally imposed ends. In other words, ethically inspired decisions cannot postulate the abstract conceptual unity of *the* plant; they must, rather, take into account the uniqueness of each growing being with its temporality and non-generalizable existential possibilities.

The emphasis on singularity means that ethical worries will not go away after normative philosophers and bioethicists have delineated their sets of definitive guidelines for human conduct. More specifically, concerns regarding the treatment of plants will crop up again and again, every time we deal with a distinct vegetal kind or community.

In Hans-Christian Andersen's fairytale, "The Princess and the Pea," the true identity of a princess is discovered after she spends a torturous night atop twenty mattresses and twenty featherbeds, with a single pea lodged underneath this pile. The desire to eat ethically is, perhaps, akin to this royal sensitivity, as some would argue that only those who do have enough food to select, in a conscious manner, have the luxury of fretting about their dietary patterns. But there is a more charitable way to interpret the analogy.

Ethical concerns are never problems to be resolved once and for all; they make us uncomfortable and sometimes, when the sting of conscience is too strong, prevent us from sleeping. Being disconcerted by a pea to the point of unrest is analogous to the ethical obsession, untranslatable into the language of moral axioms and principles of righteousness. Ethics on a pea refrains from making fully assured pronouncements on how best to treat the specimen of *Pisum sativum*, or any other plant, for that matter. An ethics such as this does not rest on the laurels of its achievements but is called upon to respond, each time anew, to the ultimately irresolvable question, "How, in thinking and eating, to say *yes* to plants?"

6. Is plant liberation on the menu?

Although recent studies in botany are certainly groundbreaking, both Western and non-Western philosophers have been aware of what we may now refer to as "plant subjectivity" for millennia. Most famously, Aristotle postulated the existence of a vegetal soul with its capacities for reproduction, growth, and nourishment, as the most basic stratum of life. For Aristotle, all living beings, including animals and humans, are alive by virtue of sharing this rudimentary vitality with plants. Other levels of the psyche–the sensory and the rational–then presuppose the presence of a vegetal soul for their proper functioning and actualization.

Contemporary research into plant intelligence, spearheaded by Anthony Trewavas (University of Edinburgh), Stefano Mancuso (University of Florence) and Richard Karban (University of California, Davis), among others, complicates this tripartite division. For example, studies have found evidence of "deliberate behavior" in plants: foraging (note that the botanists themselves use this word usually associated with animal behavior) for nutrients, the roots can drastically change their branching pattern when they detect a resource-rich patch of soil,[12] or they can grow so as to avoid contact with the roots of other members of the same species, in order to prevent detrimental competition.[13] To be sure, plants are not capable of deliberation or of making decisions in the human sense of the term. But they do get involved with their environments and with one another in ways that are incredibly sophisticated, plastic and responsive–in a word, intelligent.

This is why it is a blatant mistake to equate plants with machines. The mistake itself has a long history, parallel to the

---

12. A. H. Fitter, "The Topology and Geometry of Plant Root Systems: Influence of Watering Rate on Root System Topology in *Trifolium pretense*," *Annals of Botany*, 58(1), pp. 91-101.

13. B.E. Mahall and R.M. Callaway, "Root Communication among Desert Shrubs," *PNAS*, 88(3), pp. 874-6.

Cartesian treatment of animal and human bodies as automatons. We cannot rid ourselves of such preconceptions overnight: the plant-as-machine metaphor has become so entrenched that it is difficult to digest evidence to the contrary. In the age of communication technologies, it makes sense to compare plants to certain "intelligent," information-processing machines, for instance, computers or cellphones. Nonetheless, chemical signaling conducted through plant roots is not comparable to the waves emitted and received by cellphones. The study by scientists from the Blaustein Institute for Desert Research, which I cited in the original article,[14] included a report on the enhanced ability of common pea plants, recipients of biochemical communication, to withstand drought, even when they did not directly experience this abiotic stress-inducer. I doubt that a cellphone would learn to function better on a low battery if it had previously received a message from another cellphone in a similar predicament.

How do these new findings bear upon dietary ethics? First, they do not mean that we should stop eating plants. Rather, the idea is not to reduce plants to the storehouses of carbohydrates and vitamins or to that other source of energy so widely applauded today, biofuel. Respect for vegetal life entails nurturing all the potentialities proper to it, including those unproductive from the human point of view. It is especially pernicious to grow plants from sterile seeds, already robbed of their reproductive potential, patented and appropriated by profit-driven enterprises. Not only do these agricultural "innovations" harm farmers, who are forced to buy seeds every year from multinational corporations, but they also violate the capacity for reproduction at the core of the Aristotelian vegetal soul.

Given the co-evolution that brought together plants and humans, we are more interdependent with the world of vegetation, in the very depths of our being, than we realize. "We are what we eat" rings even truer now that Chinese

14. See the previous chapter in this book.

researchers discovered that molecules of rice survive the digestion process, enter the blood stream of animals and regulate the expression of mammalian genes.[15] Violence against plants backfires, as it leads to violence against humans and against the environment as a whole, for instance when plants are genetically modified and made resistant to insects, pests or diseases. Minimally, then, respect for whatever we eat must filter through human self-respect, as the eaten becomes a part of who or what we, ourselves, are.

The ensuing dietary ethics does not imply that we should start eating more animal flesh or, for people who are neither vegans nor vegetarians, continue consuming it in good conscience. Plant stress does not reach the same intensity and does not express itself the same way as animal suffering—a fact that must be reflected in our practical ethics. And yet, the commendable desire to ameliorate the condition of animals, currently treated as if they were meat-generating machines, does not justify strategic argumentation in favor of the indiscriminate consumption of plants. The same logic ultimately submits the bodies of plants, animals and humans to total instrumentalization by pitting them against an abstract and rational mind. It follows that the struggles for the emancipation of all instrumentalized living beings should be fought on a common front.

The project of plant liberation, as I see it, would allow plants to be what they are and to realize their potentialities, often in the context of cross-kingdoms co-evolution. Inasmuch as humans and animals share the vegetal soul with plants, the potentialities of the latter are also ours, even if, frequently, we fail to recognize them as such. Since the nutritive capacity is part and parcel of vegetal life, questions regarding dietary ethics are crucial to this project. We cannot subsist on inorganic matter alone, as plants do, but we can critically question our dietary choices without prescribing a perfectly violence-free and universally applicable way of eating. A mindful dietary

---

15. Lin Zhang, et al. "Exogenous Plant MIR168a Specifically Targets Mammalian LDLRAP1: Evidence of Cross-Kingdom Regulation by microRNA," *Cell Research* 22 (2012), pp. 107-26. DOI: 10.1038/cr.2011.158.

pattern would combine distinct parts of the Aristotelian soul: the nutritive capacity, which forms the vegetal heritage in us, and the reasoning capacity, which Aristotle deemed to be properly human. And, when it does, plant liberation will finally be on our moral menus.

7. Plant ethics, redux

When I penned an op-ed titled "If Peas Can Talk, Should We Eat Them?" for "The Stone" section of *The New York Times*, I did not expect that it would stir as much controversy as it did in the following weeks. My argument was attacked by everyone from Christian fundamentalists to vegans and from neuroscientists to humanist rationalists. Since then I have responded to some of the criticisms in another *Times* piece, "Is Plant Liberation on the Menu?" and participated in a debate on plant ethics with animal rights advocate, Gary Francione.[16] Despite the occasionally heated polemics, I take the interest in this topic to be an encouraging sign that the current attitudes toward plants may be starting to shift. The sheer fact that they can become the subjects of intense discussion and debate implies that plants do not have to be forever confined to the inconspicuous background of our everyday lives.

It seems, however, that all this is but the tip of an iceberg now emerging from the stagnant waters of humanist ethics. Even a cursory consultation with the findings of contemporary botany is enough to gauge how they are rapidly dismantling what we thought we knew about plants. Not only can some plants defend themselves by releasing volatile chemicals that attract the predators of the very herbivores who feed on them[17] but they can also differentiate between members of the same species and "strangers," altering their root growth in response to the identity of the neighboring plant.[18]

At the moment, our political and ethical thinking about vegetation is lagging behind these discoveries. Most people believe that plants border on machines, wholly determined

---

16. See the preceding chapter and the final text in the present book.

17. Paul Paré and James Tumlinson, "Plant Volatiles as a Defense against Insect Herbivores", *Plant Physiology*, 121(2), October 1999, pp. 325-332.

18. Meredith Biedrzycki and Harsh P. Bais, "Kin Recognition in Plants: A Mysterious Behavior Unsolved", *Journal of Experimental Botany*, 61(15), 2010, pp. 4123-8.

by external factors. And nothing is more conducive to the deepening global environmental crisis than the complacent and un-problematized equation of trees with raw materials, available for unlimited human consumption.

In a recent debate, Francione compared a plant to an inanimate thing, a bell triggered from the outside. Clearly, if one adheres to an ethical program inspired by nineteenth-century utilitarianism, one would want to convey a nineteenth-century idea of what a plant, as opposed to an animal, is. The yearning of some vegans to enforce the conceptual dividing lines between sentience and non-sentience prompts them to blur the obvious distinctions between living plants and inanimate things. Although they can be chemically manipulated into blossoming or delayed in the process of ripening, plants and their parts are growing beings, whose hormonal, biochemical, and cellular processes remain, to this day, largely unknown to us. Overlooking this complexity results in a thinking that is simplistic. Worse yet, it gives *carte blanche* to the forces of agro-capitalism bent on commodifying every aspect of human and nonhuman lives.

The challenge is to initiate a dialogue between the scientific and the philosophical issues related to plant life, without allowing prejudice to creep into either. In this respect, the fundamental philosophical questions are: How are we to think through the foundations for ethical thought and action? And is this foundationalist approach still justifiable, relevant, or useful? Are we to treat ethically only those living beings that most resemble us, i.e., sentient animals? Is empathy the ultimate basis for determining how to respond to someone or something? Or, is an ethics of difference (or otherness) needed so as to account for our conduct toward life forms that do not facilitate our sympathetic self-recognition?

I think that this last point is especially relevant to the ethics of plant life. Let us take the example of language. It would have been fair to say that, in talking about "plant communication," we merely project our own realities onto plants, if (and only if) communication were a uniquely anthropomorphic phenomenon. Conversely, if human language is just one example of what language is "as such," as Benjamin, Gadamer, and Derrida have insisted in the course of the twentieth century, then this manner of speaking is not a careless projection of our artifacts onto the nonhuman world but a definitive departure from a narrowly anthropocentric paradigm. The language of plants may be alien to that of humans, but it is a language nevertheless—one that appears on the horizon of the ethics of otherness.

Without a doubt, the questioning of what plants are and how we should treat them is perceived as threatening by members of various interest groups. I have already touched upon the adverse reaction on the part of certain vegans, which is, to my mind, inexplicable, given that they had to deal with similar criticisms occasioned by their attempts at the extension of legal and other rights to animals. Here is a comparison of the most common attacks on proponents of animal ethics and plant ethics, respectively:

1. Why should we care about animals, when humans are dying of hunger and genocide?

   Why should we care about plants, when animals are suffering and are killed for food?

2. Because animals are not rational beings, their lives are impoverished and less valuable, compared to those of humans.

   Because plants are not sentient beings, their lives are impoverished and less valuable, compared to those of animals.

3. Where do we draw the line if we admit animals into our moral considerations? Will plants be next?

   Where do we draw the line if we admit plants into our moral considerations? Will bacteria be next?

If, in each of these cases, the critic fails to give either animals or plants their due, it is because these and all other beings are slotted into an objectively fixed hierarchy with humanity at its apex. (For some, the Supreme Being remains God who presides over the rest of the ladder of beings. Christian fundamentalists who pour their scorn on plant ethics do so because it challenges the rigid theological order wherein plants are inferior, and, hence, contradicts the word of God.) It does not occur to the adherents to hierarchies of being and value that the categories comprising them are not discrete and that, for instance, something of animal and plant natures survives in humans.

Compared to the horrific abuse of animals, which has intensified with the industrialization of agriculture, our comportment toward plants is less disturbing because, after all, a felled tree does not scream in pain as a slaughtered pig does. But this does not mean that the ongoing exploitation of plant life ought to be condoned. To call attention to our otherwise unbridled instrumentalization of vegetation is not to argue that animals should continue to suffer in industrial farm settings and slaughterhouses, as well. This is a *non sequitur*—a conclusion that does not follow from the preceding premise and an appalling piece of fallacious thinking. The activists who think that awakening to the unlimited violence perpetrated against plants is a distraction from their concern for animals are the unfortunate victims of this crude fallacy.

Plant ethics is not in competition to be a "pet cause" with animal ethics; the main idea behind it is that the choices we did not deem either moral or immoral in the past are laden with serious consequences for everything (and everyone) affected. Indeed, the dismantling of the hierarchies of being and value wreaks havoc in a dogmatically ordered ontological and moral universe of philosophy still insufficiently suffused with the spirit of criticism. Such deconstruction does not, however, culminate in the erasure of differences between and within all beings but in the exact opposite: a proliferation of difference outside the confines of its hierarchical arrangement.

The other source of anxiety lies hidden in the responses of neuroscientists, who have long reduced human consciousness to a series of cellular and molecular interactions. As we know, plants do not have a central nervous system but this does not prevent them from sending complex bio-chemical messages, for instance, through their roots and altering their growth patterns as a result. Evidence for the non-metaphorical memory of light residing in plant leaves[19] adds insult to the injury suffered by the argumentation that still bets on the exceptionalism of the central nervous system. In other words, when consciousness is wholly embedded in its biochemical substratum, it becomes increasingly indistinguishable from the cellular and molecular processes of other, presumably nonconscious organisms, such as plants. The freedom (or plasticity) of plants is the obverse of the deterministic stricture, into which neuroscience has forced the grounds for human conduct.

The dialogue between the defenders and detractors of plant life is nothing new. In Ancient Greece, a tremendous conceptual-methodological gap was evident between the thought of Aristotle and that of his best-known student, Theophrastus. Among other writings, Aristotle bequeathed to us detailed studies of animals and their "parts," while Theophrastus left behind voluminous works, including *Enquiry into Plants* and *De Causis Plantarum*. The lineage Western philosophy followed was unapologetically Aristotelian, in that it privileged the animal understanding of humans, variously defined as "political animals" or "animals endowed with *logos* (reason, speech, etc.)." But what if subsequent philosophers were to

19. Rebecca Boyle, "Can Plants Think?" *Popular Science*, July 15, 2010. <http://www.popsci.com/science/article/2010-07/study-unveils-plant-nervous-system-illuminating-how-plants-remember-and-react>

pursue a Theophrastean line of thinking, focusing on the vegetal heritage in us? What if they were to pay just a fraction of the attention Theophrastus devoted to plant species and life processes? Perhaps, in that case, the idea of plant ethics would not have sounded so outlandish to professional academics and members of the general public alike, steeped, whether consciously or not, in the Aristotelian tradition that has become a part of our common sense. We, philosophers, should hear in the results of current plant intelligence studies in botany a wakeup call, prompting us to imagine the contours of this other kind of thinking that has much to learn about and from plants.

8. The time is ripe for plant rights

The Universal Declaration of Human Rights was adopted by the UN General Assembly more than six decades ago, on December 10, 1948. It was formulated as a direct response to the atrocities of the Second World War that brought home, in the starkest manner imaginable, the fragility and violability of human beings. The codification of human rights in international law meant to provide legal protections that would compensate for the vulnerabilities engrained in the human condition. In fact, the more vulnerable a person, the more her or his rights need to be protected, which is why eleven years to the day after the 1948 vote, the UN adopted Resolution No. 1386, *A Declaration of the Rights of the Child*.

In response to another, more protracted war, this time waged against the environment, it is time to raise the question of rights once again. Are humans the sole living beings who merit rights? What about animals? Or plants? Or microbes, as critics fond of the "slippery slope" accusations will quickly add?

The case for plant rights is, paradoxically, both straightforward and complicated. There is no doubt that plants are some of the most vulnerable living beings on the planet: even according to fairly conservative estimates, one in every five plant species is currently on the brink of extinction. Given this disastrous global situation, the protection of their rights could serve as a useful legal mechanism for decelerating the loss of biodiversity and mitigating the destruction of the flora, the cornerstone of any natural environment.

To most, the very idea of plant rights sounds fanciful. In many corners of academia as much as outside its ivory tower, plants are understood as little more than photosynthesizing green machines—those quasi-things passively embedded in the places of their growth. We are firewalled by a stubborn preconception that prevents us from updating our view of plants based on their surprising and recently discovered behavioral features, adaptational ingenuities, developmental plasticity, and so forth. Deep psychological resistance prompts us to dismiss the mounting scientific evidence that dismantles readymade conceptual molds, into which plants have been forced thus far. The default framework for thinking about plants ensures both an outright dismissal of proposals to grant them rights and a perpetuation of the unsustainable status quo, which sees the most vulnerable creatures exposed to unlimited violence.

While plants have evolved highly sophisticated defense mechanisms in response to droughts or herbivores over hundreds of millions of years, they are powerless in the face of the human onslaught. (M.N. Shyamalan's 2008 movie *The Happening* imagined a nightmare scenario where trees managed to produce airborne toxins that caused humans who inhaled them to commit suicide. Not so different from natural insect repellents plants indeed synthesize, the toxins represented a newly gained power of trees to repay our assault on the environment by turning themselves into biochemical weapons.) An extension of rights to the flora would, at minimum, curtail our negative impact on plant life. Even so, purely instrumental reasoning in favor of plant rights is far from sufficient; in addition to protecting woodlands and wildflowers as finite precious resources and increasingly as rarities, it is necessary to rethink the status of plants not only as objects to be protected but also as subjects to be respected.

The unstated foundation for the legal-philosophical concept of a right is the subjectivity–i.e., the agency or the capacity to actively shape the world–of those who enjoy the protections it guarantees. A celebrated twentieth-century political theorist Hannah Arendt prompts us to carefully examine what she calls "the right to have rights" as the precondition for the elaboration of human rights. For Arendt, this fundamental meta-right involves citizenship or membership in a political community, denied to stateless people. On a deeper level, however, the right to have rights postulates a clear baseline that makes subsequent discussions of the issue meaningful. It requires that rights-bearers be citizens and, hence, human subjects.

The advantage of the Arendtian formulation is that it uncouples the notion of rights from the corresponding idea of responsibilities. A newborn infant is immediately granted both human rights and those of a child without anyone expecting her to repay this privilege at the moment when she, unbeknownst to her, is enjoying it. One might argue that the time of reckoning is merely deferred until the infant's coming of age, when, as an adult that she already potentially is, she can both assume responsibilities and recognize the rights of others. Having said that, the unconditional foundation of basic rights overrides the logic of exchanging them for responsibilities, whether they are present or future. The right to have rights is won by virtue of being rather than acting in a particular way. In other words, it is ontological, not pragmatic!

I will not recount here the history of a laudable and still ongoing campaign by animal rights activists to ensure the recognition of these non-human living beings as legal subjects. Suffice it to say that what is at stake in that struggle is negotiating a more inclusive baseline for the right to have rights, namely sentience and the ability to feel pain. Animal rights do not presuppose any corresponding responsibilities: when I recognize a mountain wolf's right to life, I do not thereby demand that the wolf act responsibly and considerately to the deer or, in fact, the humans it encounters on its path. Nor do I, in granting rights to animals, humanize them—something that is easier to accomplish when dealing with a pet Schnauzer than with a wolf in the wild. Rather, I uphold the special nature of their subjectivity, which is not "poorer" or "more deficient" than that of humans simply because animals are not likely to entertain abstract thoughts. If, in taking seriously the insights of certain philosophers of the immanence of life, such as Spinoza or Nietzsche, we postulate an uninterrupted continuum spanning sentience and emotion on the one hand and cognition on the other, then what is required is not a radical break with animal rights so much as a relatively minor adjustment in the philosophical allocation of rights. In raising the question "Should plants have rights?" my goal is to show that an affirmative answer to this query necessitates the kind of fine-tuning which is analogous to the one that brought about the idea of animal rights.

Now that botanists, cell biologists, and plant ecologists are presenting their scientific findings on the complexities of plant behavior, it is time to renegotiate the baseline of rights once more. As Anthony Trewavas, of the Institute of Cell and Molecular Biology at the University of Edinburgh, put it in his pioneering article on plant intelligence: "If there are about 15 environmental factors acting in differing degrees and affecting the perception of each other then the combination of possible environments in which any individual can find itself and to which it must respond is enormous."[20]

Plants clearly do not grow haphazardly; they display tremendous developmental plasticity, congruent with their inclusion in the notion of subjectivity. They act upon the milieu of their growth by controlling the microbial fauna of the roots, summoning through airborne biochemical cues the predators of the herbivore insects that threaten them, or regulating root volumes in response to the identities of their neighbors. Plants calculate and follow with their roots the optimal itinerary toward unevenly distributed belowground resources; place clonal offspring, or ramets, in spots most propitious for their growth and development; and detect the difference between mechanical damage inflicted on their leafs and a herbivore attack, communicating this information to the unaffected parts of the same plant. They share information on adverse environmental conditions, communicated through biochemical cues released by the roots and initiate a complex morphological and physiological response to these conditions that involves roughly forty genes. A thick, substantive notion of plant rights will not be possible unless it

20. Anthony Trewavas, "Aspects of plant intelligence," *Annals of Botany* 92 (2003), pp. 1-20.

grounds the fresh variation on the right to have rights in the uniqueness of vegetal subjectivity.

While, in the West, scientific and philosophical debates on the status of plants are only commencing, Eastern religions have been at the forefront of protecting plant life for millennia. Several strands of Hinduism apply the idea of *ahimsa* (nonviolence) to all living beings, both animals and plants. So, in its ascetic form, Jainism prohibits the consumption of root vegetables, as roots are believed to house the souls of plants.

The Swiss Federal Ethics Committee on Non-Human Biotechnology (ECNH) 2008 report, *The Dignity of Living Beings with Regard to Plants. Moral Consideration of Plants for Their Own Sake,* was a crucial Western step toward the formulation of plant rights. Framed in ethical terms, the report fell short of referring to the rights of plants, though it paved the way to the political consideration of their "dignity." Needless to say, the Swiss Committee did not deliberate on the right to have rights and the underlying structures of subjectivity presupposed in the thick account of vegetal life either. Still, *The Dignity of Living Beings with Regard to Plants* is an undeniable milestone, if only because it took the debate to the level of a Federal Committee in a European country. Among other things, Committee members unanimously recommended considering as morally impermissible any arbitrary harm inflicted onto plants; by majority decision required that a moral justification be provided whenever plants are subject to total instrumentalization; and, again by majority decision and for moral reasons, excluded plants from the category of absolute ownership. In other words, the report advised against treating plants as things and prepared the grounds for conferring onto them the status of moral agents with the right to have rights.

To sum up: what, then, are the reasons for granting rights to plants? In classical philosophical terms, we might say that, as subjects with a rather open-ended scheme of growth and development (a scheme substantially more open-ended than those of humans and animals), they possess intrinsic worth, pursue a good of their own, and thus merit respect. Plants do not exist exclusively for animal and human consumption; on the contrary, they had already flourished long before we made our appearance onto the evolutionary scene. This is the fundamental reason for entertaining the possibility of plant rights. A more pragmatic justification hinges on the need to protect some of the most vulnerable living beings on the planet. The evolutionary success of plants and their tenacity could be offset by human destruction of the flora on a scale unparalleled by any other species. The discourse of rights would then be one among many legal tools intended to set limits on the enormous footprint we are leaving on plant and animal populations around the world.

Formulating a possible *Universal Declaration of Plant Rights* will require a great deal of interdisciplinary work, involving plant biologists, philosophers, bioethicists, and legal scholars, among others. All I can do here is hint at the principles likely to underpin these discussions. The right to flourish would be congruent with the respect paid to the vegetal potentialities of growth and reproduction. In concrete terms, it would imply a ban on genetic manipulation resulting in sterile seeds that robs plants of their potentialities and harms farmers, forced to repurchase seeds from multinational corporations in every agricultural cycle. The right to be free of arbitrary violence and total instrumentalization would acknowledge the plants' intrinsic value and, as a result, set limits on their utilization for external ends. It would mean, for instance, imposing severe restrictions on logging practices and making wanton destruction of vegetation a violation of plant rights. These two principles would spell out the facets of positive and negative freedom as it applies to plant life.

The all-too-prevalent abuses of human rights around the world should not be wielded as an argument against the extension of rights to non-human living beings. It is tragic that every day countless people suffer from torture, slavery, or arbitrary arrest, yet neither this suffering nor the attempts to ameliorate it justify an indiscriminately violent treatment of other kinds of life. Martin Luther King, Jr. famously wrote in a letter from Birmingham Jail, "Injustice anywhere is a threat to justice everywhere." Whether explicitly or not, the maximalist thrust of Dr. King's principle informs every struggle for legal rights, including that waged on behalf of plants.

9. How plants lead us beyond organismic logic

Since the second half of the nineteenth century, European thinkers have been rebelling against the totalizing worldview that reached its crest in the philosophy of Hegel. Nietzsche and Kierkegaard used fragmentation and absolute singularity as part of their arsenal in the struggle against the totality. In twentieth-century French thought, this drive continued unabated. Levinas appealed to the infinity of the Other; Deleuze favored a series of becomings that signaled the disintegration of "molar" structures; and Derrida heralded deconstruction as a way (or a no-way: *aporia*) of suspending the operations of analysis and synthesis.

But here is the problem, as I see it. Whilst philosophers were waging battle against totality, empirical scientists were busy dissolving its biological instantiation in organismic units into a multitude of biochemical reactions, biophysical properties, and algorithmic-computational processes. By the time this dissolution was complete, there was no longer any living totality to oppose. The philosophers' squabbles appeared as nothing more than a quixotic fight against windmills and phantasms. And botany was one of the notable casualties of the scientific revolution, which supplanted it with "plant sciences." A staple of that discipline, the morphological study of vegetal forms became a thing of the past. *Botanical* is now meaningful only as a designation in the history of science or an indication of vegan food items on restaurant menus.

Is scientific reductionism a better alternative to organismic categories? Should we welcome any sort of fragmentation or de-totalization? Doesn't the loss of the most important figure of individuation in biology (namely, the organism) carry negative consequences for the ethics of our engagement with the worlds of non-human living beings that surround and inhabit us? For, what is to be respected in networks of hormonal transduction or bioelectrical signaling that happens in certain organic tissues and cells?

There are no easy solutions to these quandaries. Our nostalgia for organismic integrity would be as misplaced as an enthusiastic acceptance of contemporary scientific reductionism. The task before us is to discover a biological mode of individuation that would be neither bewitched by the logic of the organism nor would subscribe to a complete disintegration and *nano*-mechanization of the world.

The fate of plants that, processed by the relevant sciences, lose all recognizable shape is shared by all living beings, including human and non-human animals. As far as most scientists are concerned, their (and our) coherent outlines disappear and what remains in the wake of forms are material processes, into which the living have been analyzed. More often than not, in the aftermath of this overzealous destruction of the whole, integrative functions and their corresponding structures are a matter of intense speculation and debate, especially in the case of plant behavior. Like strands of Anglo-American philosophy known as "analytic," most of the sciences today succumb to a one-sided method lacking the moment of synthesis. There is no simple recipe for putting back together in thought the parts, into which scientists have disassembled organic and inorganic entities alike. (Even in the circles of non-analytic philosophy, the heavy emphasis placed on "criticism," either of a textual or of a conceptual variety, often loses track of affirmative thinking, which is not synonymous with mere acquiescence.) Ecology is an exception to this trend, precisely because it considers living beings in interaction with each other and with their milieu, giving us a preview of their non-totalizing syntheses.

What is special about plants is that their status was already ambiguous in total systems of thought. In Hegel's *Philosophy of Nature* they were confined to a gray area between the minerals and the world of animal organisms. Hegel's metaphysical dead-ends, for us they hold the promise of a radically different biological individuation, the individuation that does not ruthlessly pit the one against the many. I submit that plants are both more and less than organisms; they are sub-organismic processes and supra-organismic ensembles. The scientific shattering of their *Gestalt* (their totalizing form) is thus valuable, provided that it is mitigated by a new type of relational agency—ecological, anarchic-communitarian, and unclassifiable in terms of what, on another occasion, I have identified as "species-thought."[21] All in all, decisions on what constitutes a species are reached based on judging significant certain, at times minute, differences in form, backed by the genetic component. That is our present-day variation on the Platonic *eidos*, referring to the image (the look) of things and to their guiding blueprint. But, in the absence of a unitary shape, such decisions are implausible. Contemporary science destroys species-thought, and yet does not extend a bridge to another kind of thinking. That is one way to interpret Heidegger's famous dictum that "science does not think."

The caveat in all of this is that the organisms *per se* are, also, both more and less than organisms. Human and non-human animals do not live up to the exigencies of organismic logic, because living and being a totality are two mutually incompatible conditions. We, too, are at once sub- and supra-organismic, micro-dispersed and macro-participatory, even if we still do not fully comprehend our predicament, clinging instead to the outmoded totality of personhood or individuality. Given the ground-shift in the scientific landscape where the idea of the organism is now suppressed, plants, traditionally excluded from the organismic realm, can provide us with markers for orientation on the novel terrain. They can intimate to us what togetherness in falling apart looks like at every level, from living tissues to groups and communities. They can illuminate singularity outside the constraints of individuality. And they can reveal what it means to affirm the other and the world without, thereby, abnegating ourselves.

---

21. Cf. Chapter 4 in this book.

10. Anti-Linnaeus
(or, an earthquake in botanical nomenclature)

In 2012, Vitoria-Gasteiz, the capital of the Basque Country where I work, had the honor of being the European Green Capital—a title it gained, in large part, thanks to the fact that it has "a high proportion of green public areas, ensuring that the entire population lives within 300m of an open green space."[22] It is, therefore, one of the most auspicious places in Europe today for thinking about and reevaluating human relation to plants.

Against the backdrop of the economic crisis that has gripped Europe, policy-makers have put cultural and ecological initiatives on hold, deeming them superfluous and insignificant. The same applies to the plants themselves, insofar as we treat them as ornate, resource-laden, and, in any event, inconspicuous backgrounds for our lives. It is not surprising, then, that a genuine revolution in the world of botany has gone relatively unnoticed: in its new version, effective as of January 1, 2012, the International Code of Botanical Nomenclature has dropped the requirement to describe newly found species in Latin in favor of "descriptive statements in English."[23]

In any other academic field, such an overturning of centuries-old methodologies (in this case going back at least as far as Carl Linnaeus and traceable all the way to the Roman naturalist Pliny the Elder) would have caused significant controversy and would have been submitted to public scrutiny. Not so when it comes to botany. Aside from a few enthusiasts, the public is still blithely indifferent to plants that, while stirring poetic and artistic imagination, do not stimulate our

---

22. --, "2012—Vitoria-Gasteiz", European Commission's *European Green Capitals* <http://ec.europa.eu/environment/europeangreencapital/winning-cities/2012-vitoria-gasteiz/index.html>.

23. Katherine Rowland, "Revised Rules for Botanical Taxonomy Take Effect", *Nature Blog*, January 9, 2012 <http://blogs.nature.com/news/2012/01/revised-rules-for-botanical-taxonomy-take-effect.html>.

intellection, let alone elicit strong moral responses on par with the outrage felt in the face of animal suffering. Individuals as well as groups that disregard the pioneering research of the scientists associated with "plant-intelligence studies" continue to attribute to plants the kind of unresponsiveness that transforms vegetation into perfect–and perfectly mute–material for scientific study and manipulation. Archaic systems of classification facilitate, precisely, this domineering relation to plants.

What is behind the seismic change in the way plant species are catalogued? It is above all a question of efficiency, given that another methodological modification, included in the same document, now allows botanists to publish their findings exclusively online so as to speed up the divulgation of new species to the scientific community and to prevent any representatives of the flora from escaping the wide classificatory nets of botanical nomenclature. The naming of plants is not an end in itself, nominalist knowledge for knowledge's sake. As James Miller, the Dean and Vice President for Science at the New York Botanical Garden, explains, the simplifications in the new Code make the "exploration" of each species' potential to serve as a source of raw materials, food, and medication more assured: "If a species becomes extinct before it is found–a phenomenon known as "anonymous extinction"–there is no way to explore its potential. We must prevent that from happening."[24] According to this logic, it is imperative that each plant species enter the vast system of classification, in as speedy and easy a manner as possible, receiving a name and being assigned to specific human purposes. English nomination facilitates, precisely, this harnessing of vegetal potential under the supposition that plants cannot possess any intrinsic value, unrelated to human uses.

The adoption of English as the new *lingua franca* of botany is also a sign of late, linguistically mediated, imperialism. The powerlessness of plant communities and species, turned

24. James Miller, "Flora, Now in English," *New York Times*, January 22, 2012. <http://www.nytimes.com/2012/01/23/opinion/plants-in-plain-english.html>.

into passive objects of scientific knowledge, gets magnified in myriad ways when what we do know about vegetation is coded and over-coded in dominant, imperial languages of Latin and English. Just as, up to and including the age of Descartes and Spinoza, no one took philosophy and other fields of inquiry seriously unless the treatises were written in Latin, so the contemporary production of what counts as credible (or, at the very least, effective) knowledge adheres to the gold standard of English and translation into English. This is not to say that we should be nostalgic for arcane Latin locutions that carried with them another set of hegemonic traits superimposed, among others, onto plants. Interrogating the language, whether of the old or of the new empire, in which plants are legitimately identified is but a first step toward rethinking human relations with plants, relations that are not only a matter of ethics but also of survival, for all species, kingdoms, and the planet as a whole.

The task at hand is enormous and, as such, it demands of us both patience and a great deal of philosophical and scientific imagination. Instead of devising new and ever more efficient modes of exploiting plants, it requires nothing less than a conviviality with them, a cross-species and cross-kingdoms project of living together in a community with nonhuman beings. At bottom, what is at stake is a paradigm shift more drastic than the replacement of one imperial language with another in an effort to safeguard the relevance of an old system of classification. We should strive to be still more–not less–anti-Linnaean than the International Code of Botanical Nomenclature would allow and we should do so by insisting on the displacement of the human approach to and the knowledge of plants from its nominalist base, still frozen in the antiquated categories of Scholasticism. Fraught with difficulties, this task should, nonetheless, be undertaken for the sake of extending the status of exceptional "Green Capitals" to the entire "Green Planet."

11. Botany's Copernican revolution

Did you know that plants communicate with each other through the biochemical cues emitted by their roots? That, when attacked, they produce the same substances that function as painkillers in animals and humans? That they can distinguish blue colors from red in their environments? That, for some mysterious reason, their roots emit specific sound frequencies as they grow?

The current scientific paradigm shift in our understanding of plants is comparable in its magnitude and significance to what at the end of the eighteenth century Kant considered to be his own Copernican turn. With the discovery that the Earth revolved around the Sun (and not vice versa), the original Copernican Revolution in astronomy signaled the end of the Ptolemaic geocentric model. The Kantian turn accomplished something similar for philosophy. Instead of the traditional focus on objective reality and the ontological question *What is X?* Kant proposed a re-orientation toward the subject of knowledge and inquired into the conditions of possibility for, as well as the limits to, human knowing. What are the reasons for including recent discoveries in the field of "plant signaling and behavior" in this illustrious list of revolutions?

Philosophers of biology have often insisted on the special status of the discipline among the sciences. In different ways, Henri Bergson, Gregory Bateson, and Hans Jonas have argued that, unlike physics or chemistry, biology and evolutionary theory do not obey "objective" laws, because life introduces a fair degree of indeterminacy into matter. We can interpret this claim in a trivial way, according to which it simply means that biology is not an exact science. But that is not enough: what we are after is the full sense of biological exceptionalism. Taken to its logical conclusion, the irreducible indeterminacy of biology implies that every form of life is not a totally predictable object of study, but a subject in its own milieu. Or, as Kant famously stated in 1784, "there will never be a Newton for a blade of grass."

A century ago, Jacob von Uexküll applied this insight to the worlds of animals. Even when the environment is objectively the same, he argued, the animal species that populate it selectively make sense of those aspects that are conducive to their survival, while safely ignoring all others. With time, von Uexküll's writings influenced such crucial twentieth-century philosophers as Martin Heidegger and his rival Ernst Cassirer; Maurice Merleau-Ponty and Gilles Deleuze; Max Scheller and Georges Canguilhem. But his theory of biological "perception signs" (*Merkzeichen*) did not extend to the world of plants, which remained relegated to an impassive backdrop for the drama of animal life.

Today, we are still living with the repercussions of this oversight. In some progressive theoretical circles, anthropocentrism has given way to zoo-centrism, such that animal life has become firmly established among top philosophical concerns. Without denying the value of these investigations, we may conclude that a new de-centering is afoot, this time announced from the margins of life occupied by plants.

When I say "the margins of life," I am not talking about the scarcity of plants on the planet; on the contrary, vegetal cellulose is the most common organic compound on Earth. The marginality of plants has been conceptual, not empirical, as they have been imagined throughout the history of Western philosophy in the shape of "deficient animals," or "matter organized for reproduction." In light of this millennia-old bias, the plants' transition from the margins to the center of thought would truly constitute a Copernican Revolution in botany, as much as in philosophy.

My argument does not veer toward either mystification or obscurantism; the idea that plants are intelligent living beings does not obliquely anthropomorphize our "green cousins." Such a theoretical move would only leave intact–if not strengthen—anthropocentrism, extending its effects to living beings that have been situated relatively far from *anthropos* (the human) who is analogous to the Earth in the Ptolemaic system. The point is, rather, to come to terms with the fact that human intelligence, much like that of animals and plants, is a response to the problems each life form in question faces.

The intelligence of plants is not a shadow of human knowing and their behavior is not a rudimentary form of human conduct. After all, unlike animals and humans, for whom behavior is most often associated with physical movement, plants behave by changing their states, both morphologically and physiologically. An honest assessment of the capacities of plants, thus, necessitates a simultaneous avowal of the similarities and differences between them and other living beings.

In scientific circles, there is no consensus on the implications of new research data drawn from the behavior of plant cells, tissues, and communities. On the one hand, the opponents of the Copernican Revolution in botany claim that the new data does nothing but exemplify what has been known all along about plant plasticity and adaptability. This is the position expressed in the open letter to the journal *Trends in Plant Science* signed in 2007 by thirty-six plant scientists who deemed the extrapolations of plant neurobiology "questionable." On the other hand, we have the investigations of kin recognition in plants by Richard Karban and Kaori Shiojiri; of plant intelligence by Anthony Trewavas; of plant bioacoustics by Stefano Mancuso and Monica Gagliano; of the sensitivity of root apices as brain-like "command centers" by František Baluška and Dieter Volkmann; of plant learning and communication by Ariel Novoplansky; and of plant senses by Daniel Chamowitz, among many others. Their peer-reviewed research findings no longer fit within the scientific paradigm where plants are studied as a mere conjunction of biochemical or biophysical properties. Independent of the analogies they draw between plants and animals, doesn't the drastic change in approach (from plants as objects to plants as subjects) produce a veritable Kuhnian paradigm shift, or a Copernican Revolution, in botany?

It is not the role of philosophy to provide science with inflexible and technical definitions of the mind, intelligence, learning, and other related terms that would or would not apply to the life of plants. Instead, we can imagine and work towards a creative symbiosis of philosophy and botany, where philosophical concepts would be destabilized upon contact with cutting-edge research in plant sciences, and where these sciences would, in turn, resort to philosophy in their search for an appropriate theoretical framework. Such rigorously interdisciplinary thought would belong somewhere between *a philosophy of botany* and *a botany of philosophy* with its discussion of how plant processes, as well as vegetal images and metaphors, exert a formative influence on thinking. Plant-thinking measures the perimeter of this *no-man's land* in the hopes of promoting a cross-pollination of philosophy and plant sciences.

PART 2: *INTER*ACTIONS

12. Revolution (with Monica Gagliano)

In 1999, the eminent journal *Science* published a special issue on plant biotechnology, which, according to Article 2 of the UN Convention on Biological Diversity, concerns the *use* of living organisms for the making of products with specific *uses*. Titled "The Plant Revolution" by Abelson and Hines, the Introduction to this special issue recites the glory of plant biotechnology, the many achievements and benefits of plant engineering for its capacity to deliver (questionably) healthier foods, and, most crucially, its contribution to global food security.[25]

It is puzzling that as scientists and philosophers, we would be expected to join in the chorus of bioengineering enthusiasts glorifying sameness and uniformity, while we demand from our undergraduate students to appreciate that Nature or Being thrives on variation and diversity. In the realm of biology, the existence of such variation amongst specimens and the selective mortality of individuals based on this variation are the fundamental principles of the Darwinian theory of natural selection. Shouldn't we assume that the ecosystems themselves are capable of thriving successfully? We know full well that greater species diversity ensures ecosystem stability and, in turn, healthier ecosystems are more resilient to stress and can better withstand and recover from adverse conditions. We know equally well that modern industrialized agricultural practices focused on the monoculture of uniform crops lead to unstable agro-ecosystems, which become increasingly and rapidly susceptible to pathogen and weed infestations.

The plant biotechnology story, with its less than glorious revolution, seems to point to a dead-end. The good news is that this is not the only available narrative that science can offer. The other, parallel, story (and the other plant

---

25. Philip H. Abelson and Pamela Hines, "The Plant Revolution," *Science*, 285 (5426), July 1999, pp. 367-8.

revolution) emerging from recent scientific research is, in fact, quite different in that it reminds us of how the plants themselves act by detecting shapes, colors, smells, sounds, and making accurate behavioral choices.

Here are only a very few examples. Plants tell stories of light, darkness and all shades in-between, because it is through light that they get a sense of their neighborhood and it is by monitoring the light as well as the shadow cast by other plants that they are able to determine who is growing next to them and direct their own growth. Not only are plants very sensitive to light as well as darkness, but also, by using specialized pigments called phytochromes, they are able to detect specific light ratios reflected from or transmitted by their neighbors.

Plants share stories of volatile affairs, of attractions and reactions based on an intricate chemical vocabulary that speaks to our very own noses and is irresistible for the olfactory receptors of many other animals. Sometimes, these are stories of fatal attractions when the smelly sweetness of honey-like substances on the leaf sundews becomes an inescapable and deadly ploy for an unaware insect. In turn, plants become the prey of herbivorous insects, and at those times they can call for assistance by releasing volatile chemicals that attract the attention of tiny predators that will attack the attacking herbivores. By using a variety of herbivore-induced volatile organic compounds plants can warn their neighbors of the potentially imminent attack. They are able to respond to these cues produced by injured neighbors when they are not yet attacked or damaged themselves, hence allowing for pre-emptive defensive responses. We have now also learned that close relatives will be better able to detect and understand the cues they receive than non-relatives.

And plants tell further stories of touchy feelings, like those expressed by the sensitive plant, *Mimosa pudica* that responds to mechanical disturbances like touch by folding its leaves and even "playing dead" by drooping when disturbed as part of a defensive behavioral repertoire aimed at discouraging potential predators. For others like *Dionaea muscipula* (a.k.a. the Venus flytrap), touch is not about avoiding predators but about securing a nutritious meal with patience and perfect timing. This plant snaps together its modified leaves in fractions of a second, when two of the tiny hairs covering the inner surface of the leaves are stimulated within twenty seconds from each other by an unaware crawling insect. If the timing is not right, the trap is not triggered so that no energy is wasted.

For numerous others, touch is about detecting mechanical stimulations and vibrations at a distance, as in the case of sounds. This is a story plants have been quietly whispering to us for millennia but we have only recently attuned our technological ears to hear it. They generate structured acoustic emissions, which travel in the soil and carry information to the rest of the community, even if we are still to learn what is being said. They are certainly listening to the soundscape around them, paying attention to sounds, which may be useful for reproduction or as warning signals for defense. And, no matter the senses involved, plants remember what they have learned through their experiences and, like all animals, use the learning process to adapt and flourish into the future.

Together with other stories that plants tell us about themselves, these are certainly not the signs of insensitive object-like machine-organisms. Appropriately, a theory is supported when its predictions are confirmed by our observations of reality and it is challenged, rectified, and even rejected when its predictions prove to be false. So the question that emerges is this: How can we ethically justify, promote, and financially subsidize the *use* of plants in the context of plant biotechnology and bioengineering, when the premises of this scientific endeavor are rooted in the erroneous view of plants as insensitive objectified organisms? The development of plant bioengineering, particularly genetically modified (GM) plant research, is an emotionally charged issue in society. Yet, the growing scientific evidence demonstrating that plants are highly sensitive organisms, rather than mere objects or resources, can offer a detached and unequivocally clear resolution to a much-heated issue. It is based on the state of this current knowledge that the scientific method prompts us to adjust our approach by de-objectifying plants and, hence, no longer granting scientific legitimacy to GM research on them.

At a time when society relies on scientific prowess to provide answers to the current socio-environmental crisis, applying the scientific method with the utmost integrity is a must. In de-objectifying plants, we not only provide a richer philosophical account of what (or who) they are, but, most importantly, we take responsibility for how we relate to them as living subjects in their own right. Repeated failure to integrate new evidence and correct, or, when appropriate, reject old theories defines both pseudoscience and sloppy philosophizing. To live up to the tasks of philosophy and science, we need to urgently reconsider the way we view and treat plants.

13. Learning (with Monica Gagliano)

When we contemplate the propensity to learn, plants are probably the last living beings that come to mind. They seem to be so passive, immobile, and completely determined by their attachment to the place in which they are rooted, that any of the so-called "cognitive abilities" appear to be inapplicable to them. And this is not even to mention the holy grail of cognition—the central nervous system with extensive neural networks—that plants do not have.

At the same time, the suspicion that plants are capable of learning is not entirely new. While Sir J. C. Bose (1858-1937) proposed the idea just over a century ago, it has truly entered the arena of scientific enquiry only in recent years. The reason for the delay is obvious: one widespread assumption in the twentieth and even the twenty-first centuries has been that learning relies either on the infrastructure of neuronal processes or, in the case of machines, on artificial neural networks that follow the model of their biological counterparts. With this assumption in the background, experiments on plant learning, memory, and decision-making have been construed as acts of sheer madness. But, in all fairness, while we have pondered human and animal learning since antiquity, we are still asking the basic questions about how learning really works because finding the answers is not so easy even in these kinds of organisms.

So, how would we ask those same questions with regard to plants? Do plants have motivations and preferences? Do they have expectations and, if so, how can we assess them? Do they make choices and if so, what are the implications for how we regard them? The creative challenge here is to develop suitable experimental and theoretical tools that enable plants to show us what and how they learn, while refusing to raise human or animal abilities to the standard template for these investigations.

If we start discussing the issue from the ground up, we will realize that everything we know about the world is learnt through repetition. Learning from the things that we experience again and again is, actually, one of the most effective ways of acquiring new behaviors, or of adjusting and refining old ones, in order to survive and to thrive in a range of ecological and social settings. Why would plants be excluded from such a useful evolutionary process? Wouldn't being barred from learning harm their chances for survival? Wouldn't it be utterly wasteful, not to mention dangerous, for them to register stimuli from their environments each time anew, without the accumulated memory of past experience that would enable them to respond appropriately in the future?

Like humans and many animal species, the sensitive plant *Mimosa pudica* also learns through repeated practice. Usually, when subjected to a disturbance for the first time, it instinctively closes its leaves, a mechanism designed to defend itself against predators. But, as recent experiments have shown, *Mimosa* quickly learns that to continue closing its leaves when a repeated disturbance proves to be benign in its consequences is a waste of energy. By deeming the experience no longer threatening, this plant stops closing its leaves, a behavioral change motivated by the energetic reward that keeping its leaves open brings. After all, the opportunity for "feeding on sunlight" drops considerably every time *Mimosa* keeps its leaves closed, which is something that can cost it dearly. That is where the learning processes steps in, helping the plant optimize its behavior.

Interestingly, the extent to which *Mimosa* is willing to keep its leaves open despite the disturbance depends on the environmental context. Experimental data clearly show that this plant does not simply react to the immediate stimuli available from the environment. Instead, it assesses a given situation and preferentially engages in behaviors that pay off from its perspective. The tendency of individual *Mimosa* plants to take the specific action of keeping the leaves open in response to a known disturbance is greater in limited light environments where the consequences of leaf closure can be dire. And, remarkably, the strength of *Mimosa*'s motivation to keep the leaves open does not loosen, as one may expect, when light conditions improve. These plants do not just "relax" when moved from a light-limited environment to one where light is abundant. They remain highly responsive and in a state of alertness, as if anticipating that the environment would soon deteriorate again.

At every moment, plants, like humans and other animals, perceive a variety of things simultaneously, but they learn to focus their attention on whatever they need to perceive and exhibit a behavioral tendency to approach or avoid the situations that present themselves. In this process, repetition is the learning platform upon which motivation galvanizes and steers behavior toward specific goals and expected rewards. It is not by chance that, on the basis of plant learning, we comfortably use words such as *motivations*, *preferences*, *expectations*, and *choices*, which in everyday speech we often equate to feelings, desires, and conscious comportments. As we learn about plant learning, the questions may not be about whether plants have motivations and preferences, expectations or choices, but what it means for us to know (and to accept) that they do.

14. Sensitivity (with František Baluška)

It is not just illegal, unsustainable, and irresponsible. Mahogany tree logging in the rapidly disappearing Peruvian rainforest might prove wrong for yet another reason: it is inhumane. Of course, a logging site is different from a slaughterhouse. There are no shockingly gory sights of animal suffering and no screaming, aside from the deafening noise of buzzing chainsaws. But the indifference of plants, their imperviousness to being damaged or even destroyed, is deceptive.

Common sense tells us that, unlike their animal counterparts, plant cells are immobile, caged in a dense cellulose membrane, and, hence, insensitive and incapable of producing real behavioral responses. In brushing off the very possibility of plant ethics, critics often rely on what they take to be an incontrovertible given–namely, that plants lack anything like a nervous system and the attendant capacity to feel pain.

Neither science nor philosophy should draw upon the fatuous truisms of common sense, however. Already in the nineteenth century Charles Darwin and his son argued that the analog of the animal brain is situated in the plants' roots. This argument has come to be known as the "root-brain hypothesis."

It is worth citing the Darwins' treatise *The Power of Movement in Plants*, where they state: "It is hardly an exaggeration to say that the tip of the radicle thus endowed [with sensitivity] and having the power of directing the movements of the adjoining parts, acts like the brain of one of the lower animals; the brain being seated within the anterior end of the body, receiving impressions from the sense-organs, and directing the several movements."[26]

---

26. Charles & Francis Darwin, *The Power of Movements in Plants* (London: John Murray, 1880), p. 573.

A plant will not run for twenty miles in search of food. But its roots, with their sensitive tips, will explore extensive underground labyrinths until they encounter the most nutrient-saturated location. A plant will also not flee from a source of peril. But its roots are smart enough to avoid dangerous places by actively growing away from hostile environments. So, if plants are like animals, as the Darwins would have it, then they are animals that grow upside-down and inside-out–with their brains (the roots) immersed in the darkness of the soil, their lungs (the leaves) exposed to the outside, and their sexual parts (the flowers) turned toward the airy expanses above. (There is nothing inherently wrong with this comparison, so long as we relativize what is "up" and what is "down," without treating the animal as a default point of reference. Which means that, just as plants are the upside-down animals, the animals are the downside-up plants.)

Let us agree, then, that plant roots are sensitive to the underworld, which to us, humans, symbolizes the realm of death or, at best, connotes unconscious existence, as encapsulated in Plato's famous allegory of the cave. Still, in and of itself, this claim is likely to be insufficient when it comes to convincing our skeptical friends that the carrots and radishes they eat, as well as the cacti and the orchids growing on their windowsills, are sensitive beings. Upping the ante, we ask: What if plant cells were actually more like neurons than like miniscule cellulose prisons? And what if plants felt something like pain?

Take, for example, the sensitive plants *par excellence*. *Mimosa pudica* is colloquially dubbed "touch-me-not" because it closes its leaves as soon as you pass your hand over them. *Dionaea muscipula*, or Venus flytrap, detects and feasts on the insects attracted to its suggestive lobes. Both plants lose their distinctive sensitivity, when they are exposed to anesthetics–the very substances that are so effective for relieving pain in animals and humans. The same is true for the roots of other species, not usually classified in the same group as *Mimosa* and *Dionaea*.

What is more, plants seem to anaesthetize themselves. Ethylene, a classical plant hormone which relieves pain, is released in mechanically stressed plant tissues immediately after being wounded, suggesting that it might act as an analgesic in our green cousins, as well. In turn, higher plants produce ethylene to prepare their fruit for being "painlessly" devoured by animals and humans, who will then spread their seeds. Only the mature "anaesthetized" fruit are delicious, because they are devoid of toxic substances plants utilize so as to deter potential early feeders.

Ethanol, synthesized especially by plant roots under stress (for instance, in a state of molecular oxygen deficiency) creates a comparable anesthetic effect. In response to a painful stimulus, a plant does not shriek at the top of its voice, as an animal would, but it screams biochemically. This finding should give utilitarian philosophers a pause and much food for thought.

Now, self-induced "vegetal anesthesia" is not only local. When you puncture a tree leaf, the other parts of the plant that have not been directly affected by the injury receive a biochemical signal about the threat. Having been forewarned, they can prepare themselves for the worst, and start producing their own painkillers in anticipation of the attack. Who would dare assert that the plant and its individual parts placed on "red alert" are oblivious to their survival and don't care about their own interest or wellbeing?

Perhaps we would not be so shocked to hear that plants experience something like pain if we realized that their cells, too, can fire, generating action potentials (APs). Referring to rapid rises and falls in the electrical charges that occur in the membranes of excitable cells such as our neurons, APs have been recorded regularly in plants since 1873. It is now obvious that not only *Mimosa* and *Dionaea* but also all plants produce APs, responsible for anything from wound healing to respiration and photosynthesis.

And then there are the visible approximations between plant cells and neurons, the only cells in animals and humans that, like those in plants, lack centrioles, or cylinder-shaped cell structures. Similar to the bloodless plant cells, neurons avoid direct contact with the bloodstream and, instead, are protected and nourished via the blood-brain barrier. Even the shapes and principles of cellular polarities in tip-growing plant cells–root hairs and pollen tubes–are reminiscent of neurons extending their axons.

The sensitivity of plants is not a matter of fairy tales about talking trees, such as the Ents in J.R.R. Tolkien's *The Lord of the Rings*. Far from photosynthesizing "green machines," plants are agents in their milieu, pursuing their optimal development, or, in other words, seeking a good of their own. It is up to ethical thought to catch up with the recent scientific findings about the plants' responses to damaging stimuli, search for nourishment, and avoidance of danger.

We need not adhere to utilitarianism to justify the inclusion of plants among the objects of our moral considerability. The interests of a Venus flytrap as much as those of a mahogany tree unmistakably come through in their purpose-driven, intentional, and intelligent behaviors. Their total instrumentalization, that is to say, the unlimited use of plants for human purposes, is, in turn, unjustifiable both because of the undue stress it causes and because it overwrites the interests of the plants themselves.

To be sure, plants to do not speak our languages and do not think in our zoo- and anthropocentric terms. But they are a case-in-point of intelligent behavior and sensitivity, albeit independent of a cerebral structure and nervous system. From the lower to the higher varieties, plants demonstrate that it is possible to act purposefully in the environment without leaving their places of growth and without forming human-like conscious representations of the world. They are highly social, communicative beings, even though their communication patterns are not as striking to a naked human eye as, say, the bee's waggle dance. Those who deign to speak on behalf of plants, cast as insensitive and indifferent organisms, unwittingly reveal their own insensitivity to the complexities of non-human living beings.

15. Communication (with Yogi Hendlin)

To human knowledge, it seems that the better our technology, the more intelligent and communicative plants become. But, surely, there hasn't been a sudden surge in plant intelligence in the last thirty years; it was our perception of plants that has been growing and, to some extent, we ourselves have grown with it. This leads to the question: If in the last decades we've discovered a myriad new ways plants communicate, both internally and externally, then what other mysteries remain opaque to our knowledge? And, more importantly, how can what we already know about plant communication lead us to rethink the general notion of communication?

Let us first try to clear our heads and hear what the word itself has to say. Before signifying the transfer of information, the sending of messages, or the stimulus-response model, *communication* means the process of creating a community, teasing out something in common, shared by all. At least since Greek antiquity, the vegetal principle of vitality has stood for the most basic type of life, shared by plants, animals, and humans. The capacities to acquire nourishment and to reproduce, grouped under this principle, are common to all kinds of living beings. Yet, these are the same capacities that modern science, Darwinism included, has loaded with egoistic intentionality, if not at the level of individual specimens, then at the level of the species. Instead of assembling a biological community, the principle of vitality has often been harnessed for the purpose of setting living beings apart, isolated by their exclusive interests and concerns with survival.

To recover this lost sense of communication, we ought to return to the ontology of plants, including the way they distribute resources that are required for nourishment. The method of "mother trees," directing the flow of nutrients between generations in groves (even to different tree species),[27]

27. Suzanne W. Simard, David A. Perry, et al. "Net Transfer of Carbon between Ectomycorrhizal Tree Species in the Field." *Nature* (388), 1997, pp. 579-582.

demonstrates a remarkable amount of care and sharing be-tween organisms. While the mother trees funnel more nu-trients to their own progeny than to other trees, there is an economy of nutrients and energy circulation (thanks to the mycorrhizal helper-fungi that facilitate the functioning of root systems) that lies somewhere beyond altruism and self-ishness. Indeed, it is more of a communist model of "from each according to their ability, to each according to their needs" than a system of abstracting self-interest from the in-terests of one's neighbors. Plant scientists even postulate that a plant's leaves produce extra energy so they can share this energy with other plants in the undergrowth that receive less light.[28]

If plants communicate with one another, it is because they are communal through and through. They are not individuated, as most animals are, with clear boundaries be-tween self and other. Plants simply cannot be conceived as individual organisms, but instead as subjects with deeply plu-ralistic identities, ranging from their own decentralized in-telligence—their "brain analogue" existing in their manifold roots—to their interdependent survival. On the face of it, plants' radical otherness has to do, in part, with this fluidity of the distinction between self and other. But are humans really excluded from the communal ontology of plants and, by extension, from their mode of communication?

Human relations in the past century have been misunder-stood as the action of individualistic, purely selfish, rational actors. In economics, much of our communication, especial-ly in the marketplace, has been reduced to shrewd cost-bene-fit calculations. But as David Graeber has argued in his 2011 book *Debt: The First 5,000 Years*, such exchange-based interac-tions are only guided by selfish rational-actor principles with people one never expects to see again, that is to say, in the most uprooted social context imaginable. Conversely, shar-ing with friends and community members in many societies

28. Marc-André Selosse, et al. "Mycorrhizal Networks: Des Liaisons Dangereus-es?" *Trends in Ecology and Evolution*, 21(11), 2006, pp. 621-628.

94

is a simple act of giving, knowing that one can call on a favor if need be, but without reducing favors to the quantitative accounting of *quid pro quo*. We share in order to get on, and get by. The daily interactions of plants, as well as many humans, operate more according to a gift economy model than by calculating the returns on their investments (though gifting also opens up a whole world of complications, as Graeber and Derrida have revealed).

Besides creating a community with other plants of the same species that might not be perceived as distinct from the communicating "self," vegetal communication forges communities across species and biological kingdoms. Plants marshal beneficial insectivorous insects, attracting them by spraying specifically targeted volatile organic chemical scents in order to ensure pest control against herbivorous predators.[29] As we have already mentioned, they cooperate with fungi near the root apex area in order to optimize their intake of nutrients. And these are just two of many examples, in which plants construct biological networks that are symbiotic rather than competitive, based on shared interests rather than mutually exclusive gains.

To sum up: before considering the content or the form of communication, whether human or nonhuman, it is crucial to ask the patent philosophical question, *What is communication?* Plants help us provide some of the initial responses to this imquiry by revealing that the "message," or what is communicated, is not separate from the communicating agent, which is a communal being at every level of its cellular, tissue, and environmental architecture. Much in the same way, human language, erroneously identified with communication *in toto*, is not a tool for the transfer of information but part and parcel of our ontology, our inherent communal makeup. This is, no doubt, the sense of Heidegger's often misinterpreted statement that "language is the house of being," which ought to be taken outside its narrow human

---

29. Silke Allmann and Ian T. Baldwin, "Insects Betray Themselves in Nature to Predators by Rapid Isomerization of Green Leaf Volatiles." *Science* (329), 2010, pp. 1075-8.

confines and adapted to non-human modes of communication. Theorizing plant language as the house of plant being would be an excellent starting point for this difficult endeavor.

16. Patriarchy (with Luis Garagalza)

Philosophy flourished in Ancient Greece on the basis of the idea of nature, construed in vegetal terms. The Greek word for nature was *phusis*, alluding to growth and, in particular, to the germination and blossoming forth of plants. Nonetheless, the version of classical metaphysics that became predominant in the West was transfixed by the animal world. Provoking the laughter of Diogenes, Plato characterized the human as a featherless bipedal animal and presented an indelible image of the soul as a charioteer who tries to steer a carriage drawn by two horses. Aristotle, in his turn, defined the human as a "rational animal."

Granting privilege to animals, and positioning them hierarchically above vegetal life, effectively opposes the metaphysical mode of thinking to *phusis*-nature, which is closely linked to the world of plants. Paradoxically, the most ethereal, spiritual dimension of metaphysical thought unfolds *contra natura*, against nature, which is to say, against plants. We emphasize the paradoxality of this move particularly in relation to Aristotle's philosophy, where the demand is to think each being according to what it is, in keeping with its nature, *kata phusin*. But what does "according to nature" mean, when the word is divested of its vegetal connotations? Perhaps, one can say that metaphysics thinks nature itself against nature and that, it is in accord with this de-vegetalized "counter-nature nature," that singular beings and being as a whole are grasped.

Aristotle's expression *kata phusin* actually contains a veiled double allusion to vegetal life. We have highlighted the first of these overtones, namely the origination of *phusis* in plant processes and phenomena of growth. The other is hidden in the word *kata*: *according to…, in keeping with…. Kata* implies the continuity of thinking with the matter thought about, the former faithfully following whatever the latter presents and dictates. Millennia later, this will have become the fundamental principle of phenomenology. Aristotelian thought cannot, under any circumstances, oppose itself to the object of its inquiry, and think against it. Furthermore, it has no object, considering that this construct is something posited over and against the subject, thus violating the continuity of *kata phusin*. Unbeknownst to him, twice over, Aristotle calls upon us to think similarly to plants, jointly with the environment, with the elements of the earth, water, air, and celestial fire, and with everything else gathered under the vegetal heading of growth. To think not by opposing ourselves to and hence objectifying the known by mimicking an animal's relation to the world, but by tracking whatever has caught our interest like a sunflower that retraces the daily course of the sun.

The attraction of metaphysics to the figure of the animal may be correlated to the privilege that this tradition accords to patriarchy and masculinity. Along with plants, women have long been considered irrational, lacking in intelligence, much closer to the earth and the world of matter than that of spirit. To a certain extent, that has also been the fate of animals, in that reason has been exclusively attributed to humanity, and only to its male representatives at that. Still, it has been much easier for us to accept that there is something like animal intelligence than to admit that there is also an intelligence of plants. What explains this strong resistance? Could it be due to the nature of patriarchal rationality, sustaining our techno-instrumental world, which displays more affinities to animal activity than to vegetal existence? Does a rigidly masculine mode of reasoning intuitively feel that the life of plants constitutes its unsurpassable limit? Is that why it cannot help but view vegetation as too passive, strange, foreign, and other to be considered intelligent?

Plant scientists, such as Stefano Mancuso and František Baluška who investigate vegetal intelligence, have reminded us of Charles Darwin's idea that plants have a kind of "brain" situated in their roots that detect numerous factors essential to their survival and enable their adaptive responses. Whereas the animal has a brain above, in the air, the plant has a rough cerebral equivalent below, in the obscurity of the earth. In this sense, we might associate the discovery of vegetal intelligence with what psychologist Eric Neumann has termed "matriarchal consciousness," acting from inside the unconscious and in continuity with its processes. This psychic structure gives rise to a peculiar kind of activity, which cannot be reduced to that of an animal and which, from the patriarchal-animal perspective, remains invisible or appears as mere passivity. At the same time, the later "patriarchal consciousness" separates from and opposes itself to the unconscious in an aggressive fashion, corresponding more to the way an animal's brain responds to the requirements of its natural environment. A multifaceted opposition thus emerges between acting *contra natura*, objective-objectifying knowledge, masculinity, metaphysical subjectivity, and animality, on the one hand, and, on the other hand, living in contiguity with the world, non-objectivating knowing, femininity, a pre- and post-metaphysical subjectivity, and plant life.

In patriarchal cultures and mythologies, humans usually interpret themselves starting from animality, as superior or spiritual animals, with whose mobility and projective behavior they identify, all the while striving to domesticate or hunt these exemplars. For all its emphasis on pure rationality and the enlightenment, Western metaphysics inherits this bias, sensing an unconscious need to assert its independence vis-à-vis the vegetal world, biological origins in birth from a woman, and a model of reasoning predicated on continuity between thought and existence.

Matriarchal mythologies that originate from the gathering, as opposed to a hunting, mode of life recognize themselves in the cycles of death and regeneration of vegetation, with its mode of adapting to and working with the environment without ruthlessly transforming it. Although the process of humanization has shifted from the vegetal to the animal, it need not detain itself at the latter stage forever. Its culmination would signal a coexistence of the animal-patriarchal spirit with the vegetal-matriarchal soul, recovered in the context of freedom, equality, and communal attachment. It would, thus, mean thinking according to and against "nature," keeping the objectivating drive in check.

17. Bioacoustics (with Monica Gagliano)

While walking in a forest on a sunny day, we imbibe a whole symphony of sounds: the chirping of birds, the soft rustling of the breeze in the leaves, the flowing of water in a creek... In the midst of this rich acoustic ensemble of organic and inorganic nature, the plants themselves appear to be silent. As French poet, Francis Ponge simply expresses this in "Fauna and Flora," "they have no voice," *ils n'ont pas de voix*.[30] Ponge's statement, confirmed by our experience of a promenade in a forest, is so obvious, and yet so far from the truth!

Besides the audible impressions from plant leaves and branches as raindrops touch them or the wind sways them, plants generate their own cacophony of sounds mostly emitted at the lower and higher ends of our auditory range, hence making them very difficult or simply impossible for our ears to detect. Some of these sounds are thought to be the incidental by-products of the abrupt release of tension in the water-transport system following cavitation (formation of cavities in liquids), particularly in drought-stressed plants. But many others are not caused by the cavitation disruption, and in fact, recent evidence indicates that plants generate sounds independently of dehydration and cavitation-related processes. We do not know how plants produce all of these acoustic emissions, or whether the latter contain any information for other plants or organisms, and, finally, what message they convey, if any. Yet, the fact remains that plants do have their very own "voices," to which we are only beginning to attune our scientific and philosophical ears. In trying to discern these voices, we ought to be careful not to overwrite them with the sounds that are familiar, let alone pleasing, to us. Although the "music of plants" conveys, in a very palpable way, the sensitivity of these living beings, it robs them of their own mode of expression.

---

30. Francis Ponge, *Selected Poems*, edited by Margaret Guiton (Winston-Salem: Wake Forest University Press, 1994), pp. 68-9.

Our endeavors to register the subtle movements of plants fall into a similar predicament. Time-lapse photography can speed up vegetal growth to such an extent that its rhythms would match those of human consciousness. Some of the earliest experiments in this photographic technique involved plants, and Aristotle's notion of growth as a kind of movement found its empirical substantiation. As a seedling germinates, for example, the elongation of its stem is accompanied by rotation around its own axis (the so-called "nutational movement"). Imperceptible in real time, stem nutation can be, to some extent, synchronized with the human perception of mobility thanks to a technological mediation that breaks down, spaces out, and recomposes the temporality of experience.

Nonetheless, filmic alteration of the plant's own rhythms, made to coincide with that of human temporality, is not free of violence that takes place whenever alien frames of reference are imposed on a given form of life. If we are to believe Heidegger's thesis that the meaning of being is time, then denying the plant its own time amounts to robbing it of its being.

To return to auditory perception, the allure of translating everything in the world into musical scales has a long history. It permeates the history of Western thought, from the ancient "music of the spheres," meant as an auditory expression of divine harmony, to Schopenhauer's transposition of the musical scale and instruments onto the metaphysical hierarchy, with the basses representing crude materiality and the strings making audible the highest aspirations of spirit. Consequently, actual beings are idealized as so many notes in the score of Being. It is inaccurate and unethical to answer the question *How do plants sound?* by transposing vegetal processes onto musical scales and producing "the music of plants." If we truly heed the phenomenological injunction "Back to the things themselves!", we will have to listen to–and hear–the things themselves, without drowning their voices in ideal harmonies.

PART 3: *INTER*PRETATIONS

18. Dante's Bushes and Lacan's Lilies

One thing human beings cannot wrap their heads around is a vital existence that is, at the same time, devoid of emotions. A life that simply lives without pleasure and aggressiveness, jealousy and happiness, is largely impenetrable to us if we try to approach it through the apparatus of empathy and projective identification.

Plato was still convinced that he could have indirect access to something like vegetal desire, which he deduced from the fact that plants wilted in the absence of water. Predicated on lack, desire, along with the frustration that its non-satisfaction provoked, was seen as the hallmark of life itself, of anything that, or anyone who, depended on uncertain sources of nourishment for survival.

In Dante's *Divine Comedy* we glimpse the psychological underpinnings of the human self-comparison with plants and the terror it provokes. The sentient trees and bushes inhabiting his "Inferno" weep, moan, and emit "[t]hese loud, unhappy voices" (Canto XIII, 25-30).[31] From a broken twig, "words and blood," *parole e sangue*, gush forth together (40-5). And the bush Dante addresses says in response: "Indeed your sweet words break me / Away from silence [*non posso tacere*]: let it not weigh on your ears / If I am enticed to prattle a bit, for your sake" (55-60).

It turns out that Dante's infernal talking plants are the souls of those who, having committed suicide, are punished with vegetal incarnations for taking their own lives. If these plants are allowed to speak, it is because their bodies are but the vehicles for human spirits, pieces of sentient matter that trap the souls of sinners and cause them pain and suffering

---

31. All quotations from *The Divine Comedy* are drawn from the Northwestern World Classics Edition, translated by Burton Raffel (Evanston: Northwestern University Press, 2010).

"in the poisoned shade of the bushes we are" (105-10). Simply put, hell, for Dante, is human thought, speech, and sensation trapped in the body of a plant.

Unlike the ancient Greeks, who deemed reincarnation in a noble laurel tree or an oak to be one of the highest distinctions the soul of a hero could receive, Dante highlights the inappropriateness of vegetal corporeity to human emotions and modes of self-expression. What causes the most suffering to a sinner condemned to live as a bush or a tree, spitting out words and blood, is the unbridgeable gap between the capacities of her psyche and the limitations of her body, "the tangled, fractured shape it now was crushed to" (132). A veritable ontological abyss opens between the human and the plant, an abyss not spanned but, on the contrary, accentuated by the incarnation of the one in the other.

And this gap will remain open for centuries to come, partly due to the real otherness of the vegetal to the human, and partly due to the repression of the plant *in us*, that is to say, of the impersonal, non-objectivizing consciousness that typically goes under the name *the unconscious*. Jacques Lacan will maintain (and perhaps even widen) the ontological distance separating us from plants thanks to a casual interpretation of Matthew 6:28—"Consider the lilies that grow in the fields; they do not work, they do not spin"—in one of his seminars. In *The Other Side of Psychoanalysis*, he notes: "It is true that we can well imagine the lily in the fields as a body entirely given over to *jouissance*—each stage of its growth identical to a formless sensation. The plant's *jouissance*. Nothing in any case makes it possible to escape it. It is perhaps infinitely painful to be a plant. Well, nobody amuses themselves by thinking about this, except me."[32]

Lacan is wrong: many others also amuse themselves by thinking about this. What is the image that he paints in this passage from his seminar? At first glance, the plant lives a life of sheer

---

32. Jacques Lacan, *The Other Side of Psychoanalysis*, Book XVII, translated by Russell Grigg (New York & London: W.W. Norton, 2007), p. 77.

bliss. Its freedom from necessity, which in the New Testament is conceived in terms of an exemption from work, betokens a more profound reality of freedom from desire configured as lack. It is not that the plant is impassive in the state of negative liberty, however; its "body entirely given over to *jouissance*," it lives beyond pleasure and pain in the absolutely positive state of extreme enjoyment (denoted by the French word *jouissance*), of which every stage of its development is an expression. Lacan calls this "a formless sensation," devoid of an object, and therefore foreign to the very possibility of lack, of an object's absence. "The plant's *jouissance*": is it something we, humans, can only envy, subject as we are to the pressures of necessity and lack? Is it the exact opposite of what the bushes and the trees experience in Dante's hell?

Nonetheless, Lacan does not intend to leave his psychoanalytic interpretation of vegetal life at the level of an unattainable and enviable ideal. In two short sentences, he confines plants to an inferno worse than Dante's. Delivered to the complete positivity of *jouissance*, the plant has no choice but to follow its dictates: "Nothing in any case makes it possible to escape it." There is no freedom from a freedom from necessity, from the unrelenting force of extreme enjoyment that totally enslaves the plant to itself. Uninterrupted by periods of lack, vegetal plentitude is a heavy, tyrannical burden. On the hither side of pain and pleasure, the lilies of the field are thrust into a state of extreme enjoyment and an equally extreme pain, in excess of the normal homeostatic model outlined by Freud. That is why Lacan says, appearing to contradict himself, that "[i]t is perhaps infinitely painful to be a plant"; the infinite quality of this pain directly corresponds to and emanates from the infinity of pleasure without lack.

There is no easy way for humans to come to terms with the corporeity and psychic life of plants. Neither hell nor heavenly bliss, their life must be acknowledged as wholly other to human consciousness, but also, at the same time, as the other within us, undergirding all our ideation and conscious representation. Nothing short of this double, paradoxical affirmation will lead us back to the plants themselves, beyond the signs of monstrosity or divinity we impute to them.

19. Rousseau's walnut and willow trees

No one who is even cursorily familiar with the social and political thought of Jean-Jacques Rousseau would be surprised
that he was an avid botanist and a lover of plants. It is easy to
detect a direct link between Rousseau's ideal of a more simple
and nature-bound human existence, his critique of alienation
from nature, and his search for solitude, peace, and tranquil-
ity in the meadows and the woods, where he undertook his
small botanical expeditions toward the end of his life. An
autobiographical record of these journeys is available under
the title *Reveries of the Solitary Walker*, a slim volume, which
Rousseau had conceived as a continuation of his *Confessions*
but did not have a chance to complete past the "Tenth Walk."
Having suffered a hemorrhage, he collapsed on a customary
morning stroll among plants and died in 1778, at the age of
sixty-six.

Rousseau's love of plants did not start at the end of his life,
when, as a social recluse, he sought refuge in the vegetal
world. As he narrates in *The Confessions*, in his childhood, he
witnessed a certain walnut tree planted with great pomp and
circumstance by Monsieur Lambercier, a country gentleman,
at whose estate the young Jean-Jacques passed two years together with his cousin Benjamin. His predilection for things
of nature over manufactured objects was already obvious
at that time: "my cousin and I became more strongly convinced, as was natural, that it was a finer thing to plant a tree
on a terrace than a flag upon a beach."[33] And so, the two boys
resolved to copy Monsieur Lambercier's gesture by planting a
slip from a young willow not far from the walnut tree and di-
verting the water used to irrigate the latter toward the former
with the help of an improvised aqueduct.

For a while, narrates Rousseau, "our tree so completely claimed
our attention that we were quite incapable of attending to or

33. Jean-Jacques Rousseau, *The Confessions* (Ware & London: Wordsworth,
1996), p. 20.

learning anything else, and were in a sort of delirium."[34] From an early age, he preferred to learn from plants–to the point of being enchanted by them–rather than from human educators or from the knowledge accumulated by the arts and the sciences. But the adults soon discovered the prank, destroyed the aqueduct, and uprooted the fragile willow slip.

The autobiographical episode involving Jean-Jacques, Benjamin, Monsieur Lambercier, and the two trees is retrospectively illuminated in its full significance by Rousseau's mature thought, especially by his *Discourse on the Origins and the Foundations of Inequality among Mankind*. Was the standoff between the noble walnut and the common willow, or between everything they represented, rooted in the natural or the moral-political types of inequality? Symbolically, the childish prank tried to subvert not only adult authority (i.e., natural inequality in age) but also, the power of a countryside parson, a clergyman and an estate owner (i.e., political inequality, dependent on convention). The distinction, made at the outset of the *Discourse*, becomes a little hazy here.

Furthermore, in taking sides with the common willow, doesn't the young Rousseau already display the "natural virtue" of pity, felt not just toward other human beings but toward other creatures, as well? This remarkable capacity to be moved by and interested in ordinary living beings drove him, during his last botanical walks, to pour over and study the least impressive of plants–grasses, mosses, and lichens.[35] Rousseau understood they too have the right to live and to claim our attention, which normally tends toward magnificent trees and beautiful flowers. It is this refusal to distinguish between the valuable and the useless, the noble and the common, that drove the two cousins to divert water from the walnut tree, re-appropriating it for another plant that had no rightful claim on existence in the garden. More precisely, this was not so much an act of re-appropriation, as a retreat to the

34. Ibid.

35. Jean-Jacques Rousseau, *Reveries of the Solitary Walker*, translated by Russell Goulbourne (Oxford: Oxford University Press, 2011), p. 51.

state of humanity when it still "had no notion of what we call thine or mine, nor any true idea of justice."[36] The innocence of boyhood practically coincided with the quite asocial condition prior to the rise of inequality, described by Rousseau.

Another interpretation suggests the boys may have identified with the adult authority figure, whose gesture they replicated, even if the outcomes of this mimicry amounted to a kind of rebellion. In that case, the willow as such was not subject to pity and care but only the means for undermining the "law of the father." Rousseau himself encourages this less charitable reading, referring to his "first well-defined promptings of vanity" and putting a negative spin on his actions, as he does throughout *The Confessions*: "To have been able to construct an aqueduct with our own hands, to have put a cutting in competition with a large tree, appeared to me the height of glory."[37] But this admission by far does not invalidate the conflation of two kinds of inequality and a practical rejection of property claims that ensue from one of the first vegetal episodes in his life. From then onward, Rousseau will have a much clearer idea of how to behave toward plants than how to deal with other humans.

36. Jean-Jacques Rousseau, *The Social Contract* and *The First and Second Discourses* (New Haven & London: Yale University Press, 2002), p. 108.

37. Rousseau, *The Confessions*, p. 22.

20. Nietzsche's jungle

Rumor has it that Friedrich Nietzsche's mental breakdown, from which he never recovered, began on January 3, 1889, when in broad daylight he embraced a horse that was being whipped on a street of Turin, Italy. We could, of course, see in this "mad" gesture a kind of cross-species identification of a beleaguered philosopher with an abused animal. We will never know with any degree of certainty what Nietzsche experienced or thought at that precise moment. But we might surmise from his writings the common foundation of life, shared by humans, animals, and even plants. The name of this foundation is *the will to power*.

For Nietzsche, the desire to understand life in all its manifestations could not afford to exclude either animals or plants from the overarching formula that only philosophy, rather than biology, could get at. Human, animal, and vegetal vitalities had to be viewed as variations on the same theme, namely a striving for existence. That is why roughly one year prior to his collapse in Turin, Nietzsche jotted down in his notebook: "For what do the trees in a jungle fight each other? For 'happiness?'" And immediately responded: "*–For power!–*"[38] Plato and his followers deduced the fact of vegetal desire from the wilting of plants that were deprived of water and therefore experienced something like thirst. Nietzsche goes further than that. His tacit conclusion is that, beneath a physical craving in all kinds of living creatures, we find a metaphysical longing for power. Or, to put it differently, for being.

Unbeknownst to themselves, contemporary scientists confirm Nietzsche's hypothesis in describing the outcomes of kin recognition in plants. The specimens of *Cakile edentula*, for instance, produced more roots when they shared a pot with strangers (plants of the same species, grown from seeds that derived from a different mother plant) than when they

---

38. Friedrich Nietzsche, *The Will to Power*, translated by Walter Kaufman and R.J. Hollingdale (New York: Vintage Books, 1968), p. 375.

germinated in the same pot as their kin (defined as plants grown from seeds collected from the same mother plant).[39] Perhaps, the assumption that roots engage in competitive or altruistic behaviors, depending on the identity of their neighbors, is nothing but a projection of human expectations onto non-human nature. Perhaps, Nietzsche's interpretation of the "fight" among trees growing in a jungle is also a theoretical fiction, which, in turn, naturalizes the struggle for survival in human societies. But, having said that, we ought to look for a philosophical, not a bio-anthropological, sense of the will to power in order to assess its significance for our understanding of plants, as well as of humans.

Growth, or an increase in extension, is the most physical manifestation of the common basis for life in plants, animals, and humans. This is not Nietzsche's invention; for the ancient Greeks, nature was the sum total of growth embodied in all kinds of living beings. What is remarkable is his take on power and the will—two terms that we usually do not associate with plants.

Although he depicts trees thriving in the jungle in nearly militaristic terms, their power is strictly ontological. It is the power to be, to persevere in being, without succumbing to entropy and descending into nothingness. Plant behavior, expressed in patterns of growth, and human comportment, evinced in more complex and sublimated activities, share this goal.

By seeking power—and their place under the sun—humans and plants do not merely exist; they will to be. Unlike us, plants do not face any existential problems and cannot choose to terminate their lives at will. But their willing bespeaks the intentionality of life itself, its anonymous and impersonal striving to existence. (In the case of plants, the striving is at once oriented toward the sun and the mineral resources hidden in the soil.) Our more abstract and refined wills,

39. S.A. Dudley & A.L. File, "Kin Recognition in an Annual Plant," *Biology Letters*, 3 (2007), pp. 435-438.

sometimes said to be free, presuppose this material foundation for vitality.

Despite the elegance of the Nietzschean solution to the riddle of life, the doubts concerning the aggressiveness of the will to power remains. In their willing to be, do trees have to trample their "competitors" in the process? What about the vast array of symbiotic forms of inter-species coexistence one encounters in the jungle and elsewhere? And, for humans, is living at all possible in the absence of cooperation and sharing with others? Finally, where was Nietzsche's own will to power, when he embraced and wept over a horse in Turin? Did he have to slide into madness to entrust it to an animal, let alone to a plant?

21. Thoreau's beans (and weeds)

The problem of sovereignty, though usually not discussed with regard to the vegetal world, is crisply outlined in a quandary that, time and again, crops up after my lectures. The gist of it is the following: "If I am to treat plants ethically, then how am I to decide which ones deserve to grow? What gives me the right to destroy some of them as weeds, while nourishing and nurturing others? In short, if I subscribe to your philosophy, should I just sit back, watch my garden overgrow with grass, and give up on gardening as a violent activity, disrespectful towards plants?"

In *Walden*, Henry D. Thoreau faced a similar dilemma. Experimenting with self-sufficient living, he cultivated a small bean-field close to the hut he had built in the woods: "That was my curious labor all summer—to make this portion of the earth's surface, which had yielded only cinquefoil, blackberries, johnswort, and the like [...] produce instead this pulse. [...] But what right had I to oust johnswort and the rest, and break up their ancient herb garden?"[40] If, in its traditional formulation, the prerogative of sovereignty was to "make live or let die," in its vegetal reformulation by Thoreau, it has to do with making grow or letting wither. The unarticulated basis for sundry decisions passed on plants is utility: Which species would be more advantageous for yielding food, construction materials, clothing, and the like? Whatever is deemed useless is condemned to be deracinated as a weed; whatever may serve our purposes is allowed to continue growing and even to expand.

To these taken-for-granted reasons, Thoreau opposes the natural history of a place, the plants' own "ancient herb garden," or what we would now call an "ecosystem." He does not fetishize wilderness, but implies that giving any "portion of the earth's surface" its due means, in the Leibnizian spirit,

40. Henry D. Thoreau, *Walden*, edited by Jeffrey S. Cramer (New Haven & London: Yale University Press, 2006), pp. 168-9.

respecting its self-expression, including in the vegetation that proliferates there. From the standpoint of the place itself, the weeds are the humans as well as the monocultures our species spreads wherever it finds itself or the animals it breeds and/ or exterminates. Exactly one century after Thoreau's *Walden*, Aldo Leopold will encapsulate this insight in the thesis of "thinking like a mountain."

Let sovereignty remain grounded in utility, but also let the forgotten questions *useful for whom? useful for what?* be raised. On the one hand, the weed is a plant that impedes the realization of human goals. On the other hand, and more broadly, it may be a plant that prevents the thriving of an entire ecosystem. So, if usefulness for life's flourishing, in all its diverse manifestations, were the criterion for declaring something a weed, then wouldn't vast sugarcane and cornfields as well as eucalyptus groves be included in this category? After all, the sprawling sugarcane, corn, and eucalyptus plantations reduce biodiversity, cause soil to erode and deplete the nutrients and minerals it contains.

Thoreau has an inkling about the relative nature of the word *weed*, which he upends in his self-reflexive agricultural practice: "Removing the weeds, putting fresh soil about the bean stems, and encouraging this weed which I had sown, making the yellow soil express its summer thought in bean leaves and blossoms rather than in wormwood and piper and millet grass, making the earth say beans instead of grass—this was my daily work."[41] Here is a beautiful manifesto of plant-thinking, if there ever was one: leaves and blossoms are the yellow soil's expressions of "its summer thought," concretized in beans with Thoreau's assistance. Yet, we cannot help but notice a stark contrast between his interference, or his mediation between the earth and the plant, described in terms of encouragement ("and encouraging this weed which I had sown") and in terms of an imposition ("making the yellow soil express its summer thought"). That is where push comes to shove: Does Thoreau exercise sovereignty over the crops

41. Thoreau, *Walden*, p. 170.

120

and the soil he cultivates or does he facilitate their mutual expression? Is labeling his choice of plant *weed* sufficient for counterbalancing the adverse effects of his willful decision?

We must shake off the erroneous impression that we are faced with only two options, the *either/or* of absolute control and complete passivity. Inaction and mere receptivity are the harbingers of nihilism, caught up in a deadly spiral with its opposite, namely the sovereign dream of ceaseless potency and activity. To avoid choosing is not to act ethically; it is to evade responsibility and to assume an ostensibly neutral posture, as disrespectful toward the beings that deserve our attention as the promotion of their ruthless exploitation. We cannot be ourselves *either* if we totally submit to whatever happens *or* if we are (or think we are) in total control of the situation, wherein we play the determining role. Revisiting the worry that an ethical philosophy of plants would yield overgrown gardens, it becomes clear that a certain measure of selectivity, narrowing down the possibilities of what would take root and continue growing, is not disastrous; it is an element of our entanglement with plants.

I find the suggestion that any active engagement with other living beings—whether vegetal, animal or human—partakes of sovereignty and violence to be grotesque, an exaggeration of valid concerns with the overreach of our desire for domination. Such an exaggeration does not promote but in fact harms its cause. In short, the disengagement it endorses risks flipping into nonchalant abandon, where the stance of letting-be might quickly deteriorate into that of letting-die or letting-wither. It might, in other words, continue wielding sovereignty by other, clandestine means.

As an alternative, care involves solicitude, attention to the cared for, singling out and respecting their singularity, while contemplating and setting in their context (some would say *relativizing*) the motivations behind such attention. A caring approach is, furthermore, interactive, to the extent that it includes a willingness to be cared by what or who you care for. We would be deluded if we were to think that gardening or farming is a unilateral relation; the plants and the earth respond and change their self-expression depending on my actions. Again, Thoreau is at the forefront of vegetal interactivity. "What shall I learn of beans or beans of me?"[42] he asks, teaching us an invaluable lesson in plant-thinking.

---

42. Thoreau, *Walden*, p. 168.

22. Bataille's decay

To appreciate life fully, in all its fragility, we must consider its growth, as much as its decay. While meaninglessness persistently obtrudes on the limited domain of meaning, rotting both makes possible and invariably succeeds growth. Finitude is the ever-present shadow and source of nourishment for existence.

Concentrating on the underside of plant and human lives, Georges Bataille de-idealizes both. To the ideal of beauty, usually associated with flowers, he opposes the fact that "even the most beautiful flowers are spoiled in their centers by hairy sexual organs."[43] "[A]fter a very short period of glory," he goes on to say on the same page of *Visions of Excess*, "the marvelous corolla rots indecently in the sun, thus becoming, for the plant a garish withering." The price to be paid for excessive growth is spectacular decay, whose products, we might add, have been, after countless millennia, converted by us into an engine for deadly economic growth—natural gas and oil. The erectile excess that "projects plants in a vertical direction," "in a general thrust from low to high,"[44] is powerless when it comes to maintaining the metaphysical bias of virility; the erection, symbolized by a flower stem, falls: "[p]lants rise in the direction of the sun and then collapse in the direction of the ground."[45] For all their dreaming of the vast expanses of the sky, growth and finite existence as a whole return to the rotting piles of the dump we call "the earth."

With Bataille, we find ourselves immersed in the maggot-infested lower part of the world-plant, or the Soul of All, which Plotinus both despised and wished to cleanse in his *Enneads*. Post-metaphysical thought yields to the staying power

43. Georges Bataille, *Visions of Excess: Selected Writings, 1927-1939*, edited by Allan Stoekl (Minneapolis: The University of Minnesota Press, 1985), p. 12.

44. Bataille, *Visions of Excess*, pp. 75, 13.

45. Bataille, *Visions of Excess,* p. 7.

of decay, for "while the visible parts [of the plant] are nobly elevated, the ignoble and sticky roots wallow in the ground, loving rottenness just as leaves love light."[46] The excess of growth, reaching all the way to that which rots, is due to the extreme polarization of the growing being, its tending in all directions, including polar opposites. Whereas, for Plotinus, this excess symbolized the way of evil, Bataille shows how indispensible it is for the thriving of a plant or of any living being, for that matter. Ironically, the post-metaphysical root, seeking and imbibing the traces of material decay in the soil, is no longer the withdrawn place of the One but the hotbed of Plotinian evil. The roots are mired in the rot; they are the figure of unadorned corporeality.

From a metaphysical perspective, the foundation is (the) base in the moral sense of the word: "There is reason to note, moreover, that the incontestable moral value of the term *base* conforms to this systematic interpretation of the meaning of roots."[47] As soon as the foundation sheds its false façade of immutability and begins to set root, its own growth internally unhinges it, drives it out of itself, perpetually un-founds it. Foundations rot, and only in and through this decay do they live. Bataille's thought is, therefore, nothing other than the repressed truth of Plotinus: post-metaphysics is metaphysics thought through to its logical conclusion. The emanations of the One, grafted onto a universal tree that represents the entire world, undo from within this physical-metaphysical entity.

Plant growth and decay are also significant for the enuncia-tion of Bataille's famous notion of expenditure and his the-ory of "general economy." Unconditional, non-productive expenditure, which is not recoverable either in the relation of exchange or in consumption, is the epitome of existential excess, of existence as an excessive and unbalanced (excessive, because unbalanced) wasting or spending of itself. This is, by far, not the prerogative of human beings alone: Bataille

46. Bataille, *Visions of Excess,* p. 13.
47. Bataille, *Visions of Excess,* p. 13.

sees in disequilibrium the conditions of possibility for life, all the way down to the biochemical level. As he puts it, "[o]n the whole, [...] excess energy provides for the growth or the turbulence of individuals. [...] Plants manifest the same excess but it is much more pronounced in their case. They are nothing but growth and reproduction (the energy necessary for their functional activity is negligible)."[48]

Vegetal growth *is* excess because it is pure expenditure, limited solely by external environmental conditions. In and of itself, it is unconditional and hence separate from the restricted economy of exchange (for instance, the exchange of gases between a growing organism and the atmosphere). The de-monstrative exposure of plants, the open-ended multiplication of their extensions, and their decay are in line with the post-metaphysical approach to life Bataille espouses. In *their* rise and fall, proliferation and rotting, we ought to spot *our* phenomenal appearing in the world and the rhythms of *our* tragic existence.

---

48. Georges Bataille, *The Accursed Share*, translated by Robert Hurley (New York: Zone Books, 1991), p. 28.

23. Levinas's uprooting

Emmanuel Levinas spent the years 1940-1945 as a prisoner of war in a German camp. There, he developed the ideas that made their way into *Existence and Existents* (1947), the cornerstone of his entire philosophical project.

Whilst in the camp, Levinas meticulously made notes in what would become his *Prison Notebooks* (*Carnets de captivité*), still unavailable in the English translation. The fragments that comprise these texts are quite austere, written largely in a telegraphic style, with the greatest economy of space and expression. They lack the usual rhetorical flourishes and only occasionally engage with aspects of the organic world, including plants.

One exceptional passage reads: "Tree—the most insolent verticality of living nature. Its majesty—the majesty of verticality."[49] Perhaps, Levinas had in mind Paul Claudel's poetic lines on the verticality of humans and trees, when he jotted down the note I have just cited. Or, perhaps, this reflection was triggered by another one, featured on the previous page of the notebook, where the prisoner bemoans "the fatigue of the position," the physical weight that both posits and deposes the subject, and "the necessity of changing positions."[50] The tree in its verticality is, by contrast, not burdened by its upright stance, but ingeniously supports itself with the byproducts of its life-process, converted into the hard outer layers of the trunk. What has drawn my attention to the praise of vegetal verticality is that, later on in his writings, Levinas will strip it of its physical, biological, and indeed spatial connotations, spiritualizing it into a form of the ethical relation of the I to the other. Simply put, he will uproot it.

---

49. Emmanuel Levinas, *Carnets de captivité et autres inédits. Oeuvres d'Emmanuel Levinas*, Volume 1 (Paris: Bernard Grasset / IMEC, 2009), p. 125. (This and the subsequent quotes from this book have been translated by the author.)

50. Levinas, *Carnets de captivité*, p. 124.

If the Levinasian ethical face-to-face encounter never happens on equal terms or on an equal footing, that is because the other is immeasurably higher than (transcendent to) the I; her destitution is her height, from which I receive my obligation, calling, and call. Thanks to her embodied transcendence, the other is absolutely exterior to me, irreducible to the same, such that neither this height nor this exteriority belongs to the spatial context, wherein they are immediately meaningful, but rather to the order or the disorder of time. In the matrix of *Prison Notebooks*, verticality is indexed to a plant, whereas exteriority is assigned to an inorganic natural element, light ("Exteriority–light"[51]). And this begs the question: Is ethics imbued with a commanding force only to the extent it renders metaphysical the very physical and material supports that survive in it at least at the level of language? In order to assert the unconditional right of the other, does it need to uproot the plant and its growing height? To refract light and harness its brilliance?

Verticality and exteriority, the plant and light: these combinations are hardly random. Levinas seems to be unaware of the fact that the ethical relation "without relation," as he construes it, is presaged in the plant's striving toward the sun. An infinite approach to the other, in the course of which the I will never hit its target nor reach its goal, is a modified version of vegetal growth. The I receives its individuality and uniqueness from the summons of the other, and so does the plant that leaves behind the abstract potentiality of the seed thanks to the warmth and light it obtains from the sun.

And yet, when it comes to the botanical prototype of ethics, Levinas is not quite satisfied; to the contrary, he deems the plant to be unethical! In a little known essay on "Place and Utopia," he asks: "What is an individual, a solitary individual, if not a tree that grows without regard for everything it suppresses and breaks, grabbing all the nourishment, air and sun, a being that is fully justified in its nature and its being?

---

51. Levinas, *Carnets de captivité*, p. 125.

What is an individual if not a usurper?"[52] One cannot begin to fathom the violence and injustice of these lines. Far from a solitary being, a tree is a community of growths and a point of intersection for different forms of life. It does not grab air, but gives us the chance to breathe, purifying carbon dioxide into oxygen. It does not suppress, break, and usurp, but lets flourish, enriches, and liberates many other beings to their own being.

It follows that Levinas fetishistically disavows plant life, debasing its immediate expression and glorifying its transformed, ethical appropriation. With this, he toes the line of the very metaphysical tradition he so vigorously opposes in the rest of his work. As for St. Augustine before him, for Levinas, vegetal processes can serve as no more than an allegory for spiritual existence. Allegorization ought to twist and modify their original meaning, whereas, adopted literally, transposed directly onto human realities, plants are pernicious, anti-spiritual, or unethical.

A blatant example of such a hermeneutical tendency flashes before us on the pages of "Place and Utopia." The actual rootedness of plants shores up a "horribly conservative" ideology (Heidegger, who was making entries in his *Black Notebooks* while Levinas was keeping prison diaries, goes unmentioned here, even if the jab is directed at him), which praises "the virtues of being warrior-like and putting down roots, of being a man-plant, humanity-forest whose gnarled joints of root and trunk are magnified by the rugged life of a countryman."[53] "[B]eing a man-plant" is, according to Levinas's judgment, an insular mode of being, one that not only revels in particularism but also furnishes an ontological foundation for anti-Semitism, seeing that the Jewish people are not rooted in the soil, do not organically belong to any given country. (Heidegger uncritically emphasized this same point throughout his *Black Notebooks* and other writings).

52. Emmanuel Levinas, *Difficult Freedom: Essays on Judaism*, translated by Sean Hand (Baltimore: Johns Hopkins University Press, 1997), p. 100.

53. Levinas, *Difficult Freedom*, p. 100.

In reaction to the conservative predicament, the temptation is to embrace an abstract utopia, a universalism uniformly and transcendentally blind to the singularities of places, which are always the places of vegetal growth. Remarkably, Levinas resists the vacuously universalist temptation, precisely with reference to roots, that is, by condemning the act of uprooting it instantiates. "To be without being a murderer," he writes. "One can uproot oneself from this responsibility, deny the place where it is incumbent on me to do something, to look for an anchorite's salvation. One can choose utopia."[54] The choice of utopia is unethical insofar as it neglects our rootedness in responsibility, in the possibility and the necessity of an ever-deficient response to the needs and demands of the other, the response embedded in the particular places and times of our encounters with her. Twisted and tangled, the roots linger on in Levinas's thought under the weight of a double erasure: first, they are no longer the roots of plants but of human beings tethered, by ethical obligation, to the other; and, second, the focus shifts from positive rootedness to being uprooted from one's responsibility and taking flight in utopian fancies.

On the one hand, Levinas does not want to be lost in a "humanity-forest," which grows from an overly literal reading of our vegetal heritage and is attached to the values of the countryside. On the other hand, he does not wish to wander in the desert of utopia, void of finite, irreplaceable beings and, hence, free of rootedness in relation to the other. To calibrate the difference between the two extremes, he turns to Judaism with its "difficult freedom" that combines singular responsibility with universality. All this is, nonetheless, achieved at the expense of vegetal life, abused as a repository of allegorical figures that feed straight into ethical discourse. The hidden roots of Levinasian ethics may be found there—in the simultaneous uprooting from and dependence on the world of plants.

---

54. Levinas, *Difficult Freedom*, p. 100.

24. Lispector's seeds

The unclassifiable writings of Clarice Lispector—are they literary? philosophical? both? neither?—give us almost too much to think about, despite the apparent simplicity of words, expressions, and sentence structures they resort to. What I would like to single out in Lispector's texts is the coming into her view and under her care of the world, imaged in vegetal terms. Running a little ahead of myself, I will also suggest that the missing third, the implicit mediator between her and this world, is time: the time of the world and of one's own life expressed through parts of plants and through the milestones of germination, maturation, or decay. Returning to the earliest determination of temporality (concretely, as a tempo) through seasonal change, which is also bound to the rotations of the planets and to the most appropriate periods for sowing and reaping, she grafts this seemingly archaic thinking of time onto her own existence, which imperceptibly dissolves into the growing, flourishing, and decaying of the world.

"I am tired," Lispector confesses in *Água Viva*. "My tiredness comes often because I am an extremely busy person: I look after the world. [...] With my glance, I must look after thousands of plants and trees and especially the giant water lily. It's there. And I look at her. Looking after the world also demands a lot of patience [...]."[55] Not this or that plant, animal, or inanimate object, but the whole world is under her care. The whole comes into its own, becoming-world, as she looks at and after it, patiently, with no desire to dominate or appropriate it. She does not experience the frenzy of possession but the fatigue of giving herself—to the last drop—to the world so that it would become and be what it is. That is another (ecological) way of constituting the world *as such*, without grasping, using, drying it up, draining its vital forces. If anything, it is Lispector who is drained by her constant, global care.

55. Clarice Lispector, *Água Viva*, translated by Stefan Tobler (London & New York: Penguin, 2012), pp. 53-55.

The world as such is the matter of her concern. And also a matter of time, because the world does not happen all at once, consisting as it does of multiple, heterogeneous rhythms, paces, tempos of becoming. It requires patience in the face of not only the infinite and inexhaustible variety of the movements that take place in it; not only the fragility of its coming into being that seems to vanish in the absence of an attentive and caring glance or an apposite word that says what is; but also the injunction to wait for the right time–of germination, blossoming, fruition. In this awaiting, Lispector discovers both herself, as a point of intersection for the times of the world and for everything and everyone growing in it, especially plants. As she puts it in *Learning to Live*, what is needed is "[p]atience: to observe the flowers, imperceptibly and slowly opening."[56]

Her attitude, by the way, is something Kierkegaard could not experience, according to his own ironic admission, similarly linked to the vegetal world: "I lack altogether the patience to live. I cannot see the grass grow, but since I cannot, I don't feel at all inclined to."[57] Is it sexual difference that explains these drastically opposed relations to plants, to growth, to time, and to life itself? Whatever the case, lingering with grass or with the flowers in a state of forbearance is a token for the living of life in the eyes of the Danish philosopher and the Brazilian writer alike.

Patience, tying together the world of plants and the psychic existence of a human, demands the impossible: to accompany a rhythm of being that is radically foreign to me, slowing down to the pace of florescence and dehiscence, of germination and growth. The impossibility at issue here is indispensable for life, which vibrates with its nonhuman resonances both outside and within me. Lispector, again: "This is life seen by life. I may not have meaning, but it is the same lack

---

56. Clarice Lispector, *Aprendendo a Viver* (Rio de Janeiro: Rocco Editora, 2004), p. 28, translation mine.

57. Søren Kierkegaard, *Either/Or: A Fragment of Life* (London & New York: Penguin, 1992), p. 46.

of meaning that the pulsing vein has."[58] All impatience is, in the end, impatient with the meaningless. Striving to see the growth of grass is absurd, Kierkegaard implies, and, therefore, is not worth my while. But, in dismissing plant growth, the entropy of things, climate change, the instant or the moment, the inner experience of other human beings, etc., etc., as unobservable, *ergo* absurd, I miss out on life in all its living, growing, decaying minutiae. I lack *altogether* the patience to live. The deadly flower of nihilism does not blossom on the grounds of the absence of meaning; on the contrary, it crowns an excessive attachment to meaningfulness as an ideal, which is nowhere to be found in the growing grass, the pulsing vein, the living world here-below…

If Lispector is capable of lingering with the imperceptibly opening flowers, this is because, for her, the instant, every single one of them, is vegetal. "And from the instants I extract the juice of their fruits. I must deprive myself to reach the core and seed of life. The instant is living seed."[59] The instant is, at once, fruit and seed, the end and a new beginning. Living is juicing the instant in an effort to get to its promising seed, which will germinate into another one, and another… In no way does this "extraction" involve violence perpetrated against the world nor against anything in it. Since the instants weave the fabric of who I am, the juicing of the fruit is the juicing of myself. To "reach the core and seed of life," "I must deprive myself." That is why the "small catastrophe" of taking a bite into the fruit of time is, for Lispector, always and ineluctably, gnawing on oneself: "The day seems like the smooth stretched skin of a fruit that in a small catastrophe the teeth tear, its liquor drains. I'm afraid of the accursed Sunday that liquefies me."[60]

Moistness is Lispector's favorite coded reference to femininity throughout her works, including the emblematic *The Passion According to G.H.* She also plays with the tenuous

58. Lispector, *Água Viva*, p. 8.

59. Lispector, *Água Viva*, p. 6.

60. Lispector, *Água Viva*, p. 11.

balance between the wet and the desiccated, the juicy flesh of the fruit and the hard kernel, the personal and the impersonal, liquefying herself into the written word and "drying out" her work, that is, "removing its many explicit biographical references."[61] This alternation, too, obeys the pace of living somehow, miraculously, concentrated in a fruit. Already double in itself, containing the discrete instant of the seed and the continuous flow of juices, the fruit doubles into the inner and the outer, that of the world and that of psychic life, whereby the one infinitely mirrors and passes into the other. Hence, on the one hand—the "fruit of the world," "enormous, scarlet and heavy," which remains whole and untouched regardless of her biting into it,[62] and, on the other—the fruit of her life: "In the early hours I awake full of fruit. Who will come to gather the fruit of my life?"[63]

Stated in dry (I use this word intentionally) philosophical language, Lispector's lesson is about the speculative identity between the two. The fruit of the world *is* the fruit of my life; the world is mine to the extent that it is entrusted to my care and attention; my life is the world's to the extent that it is squeezed out of me, draining into everything I do and resonating with beings that are not me, on the so-called outside. Above all, what the two fruits share (are they really two?) is that each of them *is*, so that through being (what each of them is) they come back to the instant, retracting and contracting into the living seed they harbor. The last and the first word on this subject belongs to Lispector: "And in the instant is the *is* of the instant. I want to seize my *is*."[64]

61. Benjamin Moser, "Breathing together", in *Água Viva* (London & New York: Penguin, 2012), pp. vii-viii.

62. Clarice Lispector, *An Apprenticeship, or the Book of Delights*, translated by Richard Mazzara and Lorri Parris (Austin: University of Texas Press, 1986), p. 112.

63. Lispector, *Água Viva*, p. 32.

64. Lispector, *Água Viva*, p. 4.

25. Deleuze's rhizome
(or, in philosophical defense of trees)

With deforestation claiming seventeen percent of the Amazonian rainforest in the last fifty years alone, who would have thought that trees would need to be defended from… a philosophical onslaught? Let alone from an attack that would come from the most unlikely of corners, occupied by the trendy representatives of French post-structuralism?

The writings of Gilles Deleuze and Félix Guattari have given trees a bad reputation. To put it succinctly, for them, arborescent logic and imagery connote hierarchy, verticality, and the movement of transcendence, whereas rhizomatic assemblages betoken a certain kind of equality, horizontality and immanence. Rhizomes are the modified horizontal subterranean stems that, much like seeds, can develop roots and shoots. Those of ginger, turmeric, and lotus are perhaps the most familiar (because edible) examples. Grass, likewise, fares better in the eyes of the authors of *Anti-Oedipus* than trees. It is, after all, quite democratic and egalitarian; growing close to ground-level, its blades do not entertain any dreams of penetrating the depths of the earth and of soaring toward the expanse of the sky. Inside us, humans, there is also grass, or at least the grass-like structuration of the brain: "Many people have a tree growing in their head, but the brain itself is much more a grass than a tree."[65]

It is, at the same time, crucial for Deleuze and Guattari not to fall back into the vertical system of valuation, which they criticize, in associating the rhizome, or grass, with something unequivocally "good" and the tree with the "bad." As they state in *A Thousand Plateaus:* "The important point is that the root-tree and canal-rhizome are not two opposed models: the first operates as a transcendent model and tracing, even if it

65. Gilles Deleuze & Félix Guattari, *A Thousand Plateaus* (New York & London: Continuum, 2004), p. 17.

engenders its own escapes; the second operates as an imma-nent process that overturns the model and outlines a map, even if it constitutes its own hierarchies [...]."[66] There is a little bit of a rhizome in a tree, just as there is a modicum of a tree in a rhizome; immanence is shot through with the possi-bilities for transcendence; a transcendent model can devolve into immanence through its own escape routes (i.e., lines of flight); equality can reconstitute a hierarchy; the horizontal and the vertical dimensions are thoroughly enmeshed with one another.

This disclaimer aside, Deleuze and Guattari got "arbores-cence" all wrong. The physical verticality of trees does not mean that they are vertical in the way they live or grow. Trees can branch out in quite unpredictable ways; they can accom-modate the grafts of other species; they can give rise to shoots that can survive independently of them; they can change their sexes or become hermaphrodites for a limited stretch or for the rest of their lives; and the list continues. Expressed in Heideggerese, *trees are ontically vertical and ontologically hor-izontal*. Although they tower in measurable height over and above the grass, they are as egalitarian as the most humble of plants. Given how some tree species share their root system, they can be thought of as overgrown, hyperextended grass. Pando, a grove of quaking aspens in Fishlake National Forest (Utah), has the largest root system in the world: over 106 acres, what sprouts above the ground are genetically identical trees. So, what would be the advantage of a rhizome over the roots found in Pando?

Strictly speaking, the most ontologically vertical notion in biology is that of an organism. In an organism, there is a rigid hierarchy between the different organs (some of them vital-ly important; others less so) and the predominance of the whole over the parts. Plants, as we have seen, do not follow the organismic model of development, and trees are not an exception. Even if they might be, or appear to be, more indi-viduated than other vegetal beings, such as grass, their parts

---

66. Deleuze & Guattari, *A Thousand Plateaus*, p. 22.

(for instance, branches) are not really organs limited in terms of their number, position in a body, and so forth. It may well be that all plants, including trees, are the most faithful instantiations of the "bodies without organs" Deleuze and Guattari so admired.

The penchant for the rhizome over the root derives from an understandable objection to the metaphysical obsession with depth, often associated with the hidden and *radical* nature of the underlying source of visible appearances. But the root of a tree is far from being its origin; as in all other plants, it is but one extreme in the polarization of a shoot, a seed, or an acorn that grows up and down simultaneously when planted in the ground. Whatever resembles the source in a plant is always a variation on, of, and from the middle—the extension of the middle in every direction, both vertically and laterally. "Rhizome" is a fragment of the vegetal world that symbolizes the whole: trees are also rhizomes, proliferating *between* roots and shoots.

I could add to this brief defense of trees the observation that they have been beneficial for a venerable tradition of "philosophies of immanence," going back to Plotinus, the tradition, to which Deleuze and Guattari willy-nilly belong. For Plotinus, the universe is a "great tree," on which all living and even inorganic entities, are branches, leaves, and buds. The tree is a fold—immanence, varied with regard to itself. Deleuze himself suggests that Spinozan "attributes" can be understood through the example of "a seed which 'expresses' the tree as a whole."[67] For Bergson, each tree is a society, not an individual; an articulation of multiplicities, not a living *unit*. The tree and the root are *essentially superficial*, regardless of the height and the depth they have come to represent. It is both philosophically and ethically irresponsible to turn them into villains, especially compared to the grass that supplants them in many recently deforestated areas, serving as feed for the cattle raised there. Instead of symbolically charged

---

67. Gilles Deleuze, *Expressionism in Philosophy: Spinoza*, translated by Martin Joughin (New York: Zone Books, 1992), p. 80.

preferences, which Deleuze and Guattari clothe in sloppy philosophical justifications, philosophers of immanence would do well to cultivate all plants, both outside us and in us, in our daily living and thinking.

26. A botany of words

I wonder whether one day we could muster courage and cre-
ativity enough to pursue a "natural history of words" (not
to be confused with Vico's or Condillac's "natural history
of grammar"). As I imagine it, this discipline would study
how semantic units germinate, undergo metamorphosis,
grow, blossom, and decay within and between diverse cultures. Even better would be a botany of words that would
finally descend to the literal roots of *semantics*, the theory of
meaning that borrows its name from the Greek *sema*–"sign"
or "seed." Not to mention the role of roots, among other
botanically inflected terms, in grammar! Vegetal processes
would not play the role of metaphors for the formation of
words, cross-referencing, or falling out of use, but would be
acknowledged for what they are: the first principles of growth
and decay in all spheres of life, including cultural vitality.

Before dreaming about a botany of words, we must clarify
one basic misconception, namely that the word *plant* is totally transparent, points to an obvious referent, and has an exact
equivalent in languages such as Greek and German, Hebrew
and Euskera (Basque). Obviously, this word would be everywhere implicated in the botany of words, so much so that it
would displace or supplant "God" and "Being" in traditional
semiology and hermeneutics. That is why the question about
its meanings is paramount.

When we say "plant," we immediately affiliate our speech
and understanding with the Latin tradition. The word recalls,
through the noun *planta* (still preserved in the same form in
Spanish and Portuguese), the verb *plantāre*, which means "to
drive in with one's feet, to push into the ground with one's
feet," hinting at that other sense of *planta*, intimately tied
to our bodies–"the sole of a foot" (cf. Barnhart's *Dictionary
of Etymology*). A mindboggling number of prejudices about
plants and our comportment toward them are built into this
etymology. Some of the tacit suppositions it underwrites are

the following: 1) the soil needs to be leveled and made flat before planting can begin; 2) the root is equivalent to feet, by which plants are driven into the ground; 3) plants are imprisoned in the ground, to which they are tethered; 4) plants are passive; 5) plants are, in the first instance, the vegetation that is planted, that is, tamed, domesticated, agriculturally produced, driven into a leveled terrain by human beings; 6) plants are lowly beings, and therefore; 7) ought to be subjugated, kept underfoot where they belong; 8) we, humans, are articulated with plants by means of the lowest part of our bodies (viewed from the vantage point of its physical configuration), the part that, unless we wear shoes, is in direct contact with the earth…

Many European languages have retained the Latin heritage, from the German *Pflanz* to the French *plante* and Italian *pianta*. So static is the entity it signifies that, in English *circa* 1789, the same word came to denote a factory, the installation of fixed machinery and buildings for industrial production. Shouldn't we turn to other linguistic realities with the view to liberating our minds from the presuppositions attached to "plant?"–you might ask. Beware: some of these efforts may misfire. In Japanese, for instance, *vegetation* is *shokubutsu* (植物), related to grass in the form of straw or hay. Now, that is hardly an improvement! But in Greek we encounter the word *phuton* (φυτόν: literally, "that which has grown"), derived from *phuō* (φύω), "to grow," "to come into being," "to spring forth," "to produce." On this point, there is complete agreement between Athens and Jerusalem: in Hebrew, "plant" is *tzemakh* (צמח), from *litzmoakh* (לצמוח), "to grow." And even in Russian, thanks to the ties that link it to Greek, the plant is *rasteniye* (растение), stemming from the verb *rasti* (расти), which means, precisely, "to grow."

I do not intend, with this cursory list, to persuade readers of the need to resuscitate the discipline of philology (least of all, in its traditional and highly technical variation) for the sake of giving shape to the botany of words. I only want to suggest that the different terms for vegetation are steeped in

140

divergent tendencies of experiencing plants, even as the linguistic realities themselves privilege certain modes of treating plants over others. Are we to let them grow, cultivating their own propensity for emergence and self-production, or drive them into the ground and keep them at bay? And what if the word for "plant" is absent? That, as a matter of fact, was the case in Euskera (or Basque, which does not belong to the group of Indo-European languages) before its speakers adopted the designation *landare* from the Latin-based *plantāre*. According to the explanation I received from my Basque colleagues, Euskera put at the disposal of its speakers names for particular plants (a birch, an oak, peas, wheat…) without generalizing them under an abstract heading, a higher class. Most probably, the distance from the vegetal world was insufficient *for transforming* it into an object–above all, in and through language–set apart from and against the human subject. Whatever the explanation, such a level of singularity is inaccessible to our modern sensibilities; at the limit, we can only get an inkling of it with the help of ethical categories and precepts.

Where does this leave the possible botany of words I have conjured up in the opening lines? The Latin baggage of our languages and systems of thought fixes words and plants alike in rigid tables and classifications. Together with and in analogy to plants, words are driven into the ground with the soles of our feet, as a result of our obsession with secure and immutable foundations for knowledge. Insofar as they are replaced with scientific or numerical notations, they become superfluous and completely interred in the rock-hard soil of mathematical understanding and denied a chance to germinate. We sorely need a botany of words that would discern in plants and in words growing beings, free to spring forth, to thrive, to blossom, to produce an entire world. In short, a botany of words that, at the extreme, lacking a word for plant and for word, would give a nod to the inimitable singularity of each. "And only then will words of praise arise, like flowers."[68]

68. Friedrich Hölderlin, *Poems of Friedrich Hölderlin*, selected and translated by James Mitchell (San Francisco: Ithuriel's Spear, 2004), p. 11.

27. To each philosopher, her or his plant

Irrespective of my philosophical vocation, I have always been averse to abstract speculation. Throughout my work, I have relied on rather mundane *figures* that stimulate thinking: fire, dust, plants… Everything and everyone in the world can be thought-provoking, deserving of contemplation and wonder—not a boringly unremarkable and ultimately replaceable representative of a genus or an Idea, but a source of inexhaustible singularity.

My intention behind *The Philosopher's Plant* was to create a herbarium of ideas, collecting theories of the most important Western thinkers, from Greek Antiquity to our time, as though they were botanical specimens preserved on the pages of my book. I also wished to weave a web of associations that would link certain common plants to particular ideas in the reader's mind.

I knew that it would have been absurd to put together a herbarium without the representations of the specimens themselves. To solve this problem, I did two things. First, I paired each philosopher whose life and thought I wanted discuss with a tree, flower, cereal, or grass that was mentioned in her or his work and that, in most cases, had something to do with her or his biography. And, second, I invited a fantastic French artist, Mathilde Roussel, to visualize these "philosoplants" and give an aesthetic dimension to the hybridized herbarium I had theorized about.

At times, it was difficult to decide which plant would correspond to any given philosopher. Not because their texts are virtual deserts insofar as vegetation is concerned, but because, more like a jungle, they are teeming with botanical metaphors, examples, allegories, and analogies.

Take St. Augustine. I selected pears to characterize him, because he confesses having stolen them in his youth together with a gang of friends. Just for the thrill of it! But I could have also chosen a fig tree, as a faithful botanical rendition of his life and thought, since it is under this tree that he flung himself on the grass and repented for his sins. I can already see the readers smile knowingly: the fig tree symbolizes the original sin in the Judeo-Christian tradition, according to which Adam and Eve covered their nakedness with fig leaves after eating the forbidden fruit from the Tree of Knowledge. For Augustine, both the pear and the fig are just that–symbols of spiritual reality and its "fallenness" into sin. But the pear won in the end, because fruit in general are important to Augustine as signs for the "works of mercy" or good deeds; and here was a would-be saint stealing fruit, transgressing against the works of mercy themselves.

In the case of Plato, the choice of a plane tree was clearly the most apt to my mind from the get-go. He had to be reincarnated in an enormous tree that cast its shadow over the rest of Western philosophy. Fortunately, I did not need to invent this scene, which Plato himself described (or, better, encrypted) in his dialogue *Phaedrus*. There, he mentioned in passing a majestic plane tree, underneath which the entire conversation between Socrates and Phaedrus unfolded. How did I know that Plato imperceptibly inserted himself into the dialogue?–Because his own name (which is actually a nickname) comes from the same root as the Greek word for a plane tree, *platanos*. What did the philosopher have in common with this plant? Plato's biographers offer various hypotheses on the subject of his nickname. The most prevalent theory is that he had broad (*platys*) shoulders, seeing that he was good not only in thinking but also in boxing and wrestling. Others contend that his forehead was broad. But, whatever the relevant body part, the consensus is that it was some sort of broadness that gave him his alias. Since plane tree leaves are incredibly broad, *platanos* was a suitable designation for this particular plant. As they say, it's all in the name…

The only living philosopher included in my collection is the French thinker, Luce Irigaray, who would later collaborate with me on some of the chapters in the book you are now reading. For once, I had the luxury of asking the author herself which plant she most identified with. Without a doubt, the plant had to be a flower, but of what kind? We thought that a rose could be fitting, but, in the end, the choice fell on a water lily. (Irigaray indicated several preferences, leaving the final decision up to me). Why? Well, water lilies grow—you've guessed it!—in water, which, for Irigaray, is the element of femininity. In addition to this, they bridge different milieus, emerging from the muddy bottom of a lake toward the celestial expanses above it in the shape of a pure flower. Nor should we forget that they resemble lotuses, the flowery symbols of the East, which is quite opportune because Irigaray endeavors to bridge Eastern and Western philosophies and practices in her life and thought.

But which plant would correspond to me? It will be up to others to decide.

PART 4: *INTER*VIEWS

28. On art
(with Monica Westin and Heidi Norton)[69]

Chicago-based sculptor and photographer Heidi Norton's 2014 show at Monique Meloche Gallery was titled to Threptikon—*Aristotle's concept of the vegetative soul. Norton's work almost always includes plants as formal and thematic elements; she's deeply drawn to the strange ways we preserve and present plant life. But in this body of work she was also specifically influenced by arguably the closest contemporary figure we have to a canonical plant philosopher: Michael Marder, professor of philosophy at the University of the Basque Country and author of a number of recent books and articles on the intricate lives of plants and the challenges they present both to the discipline of philosophy and to contemporary culture at large. Tracing their parallel practices of re-imagining our inherited relationship to plant life, Monica Westin spoke with Marder and Norton about, among other things, the so-called turn to the question of the animal (and how it doesn't go far enough); what could potentially constitute a plant ethics; and what the etymological differences between* nature *and* ecology *tell us about our mythologies of origin and decay in the natural world.*

Monica Westin: *I want to start out by getting the back-story from each of you about how you came to these questions. Michael, were there any particular philosophical texts or questions that led you directly to your work on plants as a philosophical problem? And, Heidi, was your practice of working with plants as formal elements what brought you to these more philosophical questions, or have you always been interested thematically in our relationship to plant life?*

Michael Marder: My work on plants does not arise from a purely academic concern. True: the thought that plants have been largely neglected in Western philosophy came to me, in 2008, as I was reading a book of commentaries on

---

69. A version of this interview was published on March 24, 2014 in *BOMB Magazine* <http://bombmagazine.org/article/1000078/heidi-norton-and-michael-marder>.

Aristotle. It occurred to me that the recent philosophical turn to the so-called question of the animal did not go deep enough into the thickets of the Aristotelian notion of the soul, which starts with the vegetative acts of nourishment and reproduction. But that is, of course, not the whole story. Much of my theoretical interest in plants is tied to some moments of my autobiography, which I recount in the book on plant life I am now writing together with Luce Irigaray, titled *Through Vegetal Being*. It all begins with the simple fact that plants are rooted in the soil, while I have been in a more or less constant state of uprooting for much of my life. In each of the places I have lived, plants have become the keepsakes of my memories, the mnemonic centers of gravity that evoke the events and even the atmosphere of my life at the time down to minute details. Allotting to the vegetal world a place close to the center of psychic life has given me a certain sense of security; the plants stayed, while I left. All I had to do was to admit them to the core of my philosophical life, as well.

Heidi Norton: Like Michael, my initial interest in plants grew out of a more personal narrative, far away from the time in which I started using them as a material. Unlike Michael, who grew up more nomadically, I was raised by homesteaders on ten acres of forest that bumped up to a quarry, our swimming pool. My attachment to, and my roots within, this landscape ran deep and would haunt me the rest of my life. As I grew older and we grew away from that home and that land, my parents began to separate from that identity. The idea of living off the land became a distant past, a myth. One summer in my studio, I painted a plant white to be included in a still life photograph (the *New Age Still Life* series). When I returned it had grown out of the paint. The resilience of the plant floored me. How could this living thing, subjected entirely to such a toxic substance (I had hand-painted every square inch) and blocked from receiving light, still be alive? And that was it. That was the beginning. At that point I knew that the plant was my material and I would search for ways in which to preserve it. The simplicity of their needs, their strength, their inherent ability to succumb—plants have been wired for centuries to withstand anything nature and time have handed to them, even ice ages.

Monica Westin: *I'd like to ask more about plants as a formal problem in each of your work. Michael, is there a way in which using an alternative hybrid form of writing about plants and philosophy is a deliberate choice to rethink plants as subjects, as living beings? Could there exist, whether or not you're doing it here, a sort of "new writing" that can speak about plants better than those that we have? (I'm thinking about Irigaray's famous work on women's writing.) And, Heidi, in describing that moment when you knew that plants were going to be central materials for you, you listed their formal properties: their adaptability, their strength, their simplicity. Can you say more about how they have posed formal issues to in your practice?*

Michael Marder: Indeed, plant-thinking had to free itself from a purely theoretical approach to plants in order to explore the intersecting trajectories of living, growing beings, both human and vegetal. Some of these changes happened as I was working on *The Philosopher's Plant*, where I re-narrate the history of Western philosophy through the flora. In that book, each of the twelve thinkers I discuss, from Greek antiquity to the twenty-first century, is represented by a tree, flower, cereal, and so on, which was in one way or another featured in her or his thought. Each chapter begins with a biographical anecdote that puts plants on the center-stage and continues in a more theoretical key, explaining the key concepts and notions of that philosopher through vegetal processes, images, and metaphors. The idea is that plants play a much more important role in the formation of our thinking, "personality," and life story than we typically realize.

In terms of Western thought, this is far from an innocuous observation, as it goes against one of the fundamental tenets of metaphysics, namely that being is unchangeable, non-generated, eternal, or, in a word, not at all plant-like. As I note in the introduction, "The history of what ideally does not grow, namely metaphysics, is told here from the perspective of what grows, including the very plants that have surreptitiously germinated within this history."[70] For me, then, it was a logical next step to rethink some aspects of my autobiography in the same light.

Meanwhile, in the course of our correspondence, Luce Irigaray suggested that we co-author a book where our experiences of the plant world would serve as a basis for an encounter–with the plants themselves, with the readers, and with each other. From the start, we have been aware of the challenges entailed in such a project, some of which you have alluded to in your questions. First, an experience *with* plants is hardly communicable. In any event, it is very difficult to render in words. That is why we deemed it necessary to invent an alternative form of writing about plants, which is still a work in progress. The more ways of approaching them one admits into one's thinking and writing, the better. In combination, philosophy, art, literature, and science can hope to touch upon something of vegetal being. So, I am pleased to be doing this interview, which is yet another way to reach out to plant ontology, together with Heidi!

Second, the plants themselves do not speak, of course, even though we can theorize the language–or better, the languages of plants–that have to do with their biochemical communication, spatial expression, etc. In this sense, the parallel with women's writing falters, because women have been historically *silenced*, in contrast to the absolute silence of plants. Still, sexuate difference is quite significant for the joint endeavor we have undertaken. Just as we can fully become human not in isolation but by sharing our differences, so too can we encounter–perhaps for the first time–the world of plants and, through it, the rest of nature only provided that we do so together.

Heidi Norton: The experience I described–returning to my studio to find a white painted dieffenbachia plant alive with new growth–created the idea of using the plant as a canvas, a form of aestheticizing it. I was completely seduced by the

70. Marder, *The Philosopher's Plant*, p. xvi.

white plant: something living that has been voided of color and life, the chlorophyll sucked from its veins, whose resilience, the new sprout, was only visible through its contrast to the stark white. But the leaves that had dropped were shells of death—chip the paint and there was a brown dead plant.

For years, I spent days upon days rushing to my studio to water the plants, to save them from decay. I became anxiety-ridden. Saving them was significant, but keeping them "green" was essential. I enjoyed juxtaposing the green colors of "life" against other colors of nature (light, water, and minerals) and those of modernity, like synthetic pinks, blacks and whites. In 2011, I began making sculptures of large domestic tropical plants literally pressed against panes of glass and adhered with resin. The resin had a utilitarian purpose, but it also referenced herbariums, pressed flowers/plants, as well as paintings, and most importantly for me, photographs. Green leaves smashed against the glass with the resin formed pockets of air, connoting plants being pressed under a slide. I made these pieces for a while, but at times the dimensionality of the plant did not lend itself to the complete resin encasement. Additionally, they were becoming too flat. I appreciated the flatness on the glass side, but I also enjoyed the explosiveness of the other side. With this explosiveness of life ultimately came death.

The brown and yellow color of decay was initially something that seemed to contrast with the voice of my work at the time. I wasn't interested in dead plants or in killing plants for art. However, this act was inescapable, and I realized my work was more intellectually dimensional when it presented life, regeneration, and death. Cycles of ecology, symbiosis, and the interdependence of nature became more prominent in my work and process, culminating in late 2012 when I mounted a show at the Museum of Contemporary Art in Chicago. I had gained access to Liam Gillick's glass vitrines, which he exhibited in 2010. His interest in social systems and relational aesthetics interested me. The use of another person's material, as well as the reuse of mine, was evident in the show. Plants that were given to me by mentors and artists, deconstructed artworks, and decayed materials were all conceptual drivers of the exhibition. I was also interested in the Museum as a place of creating, displaying and preserving.

My current show, *to Threptikon* is similar to Marder's book *The Philosopher's Plant*. I also put four plants on center stage. The plants were photographed by other institutions and cultural contributors and then printed directly onto glass. Two of the images, botanical glass replicas of plants, were loaned to me by the Ware Collection at Harvard. Here we see the plants being used as didactic material, as well as referencing the aesthetics of slides and specimens. This aestheticization is also evident with the glass cast sculptures in which the plant material, minerals, and film are encased/trapped. There is a lot of play between the inside and outside, micro and macro, and visibility and invisibility of plants and natural systems. All of this aligns with modes of vision and how that may or may not be recorded, particularly on film.

Monica Westin: *I'd like to know more about each of your current understanding of, or strongest ideas about, plant ethics. Can you condense such a philosophy to a paragraph or maxim?*

Michael Marder: It is very difficult to talk about plant ethics in the abstract, first of all because such an ethics demands extreme attention to the singularity of its subjects. I make this especially clear in the small essay titled "Is It Ethical to Eat Plants?" that I contributed to a special issue of the journal *Parallax*. For me, plant ethics is not a set of general precepts or guidelines, as those fall within the purview of morality. Rather, it is rooted in respect for each species or each plant, which is renewed and experienced differently in our encounters with them. If I were pressed to say something more comprehensive on the subject, I would stress the fact that, like plants, animals and humans are "growing beings." Plant ethics would be an ethics of growth, animated by the desire to promote vegetal, cross-species, and cross-kingdoms communities, to let them thrive on their own accord, and to affirm life throbbing in the shared trajectories of plant, animal, and human flourishing. So, it would have to be an ethics of the singular (infra-personal) existence and of the universal (supra-personal) conjunction of growing beings.

Heidi Norton: I feel plants have been long reduced to objects of consumption—whether for eating, gazing upon, gardening, etcetera. Plants are thought of as passive, things that merely sit there and absorb sunlight and grow and then die. Perhaps I am oversimplifying, but the fact remains that people who can't care for people or animals are told to get a plant. Much of what they do goes unseen; their perceived "stillness" objectifies them. My job as an artist is to point at the issues, to expose them, and provoke questions. Unlike a scientist, I do not work within set parameters, and I am not looking for empirical answers. My work uses plants to speak to instability and liminality.

I often feel confused and anxious about my work. The sacrificing of a plant makes me uncomfortable. The initial point of contact the plant has with the toxic substance or heat jars me. Am I setting myself up for failure? Utopia and the desire to commune with nature will never happen. When a plant is pressed on the glass or frozen in a photo, active looking occurs. There is an exchange of energy between the objects and the viewer: a kind of *Bewegung*, or channeling of organic energy that points at the unseen elements, systems, and forces of the natural environment upon and all around us. This anxiety drives me to make. I like being confused and uncomfortable.

Michael Marder (*to Norton*): *Does your practice encapsulate a critique of the prevailing attitudes toward plants, point toward an alternative relation to time, or combines elements of both approaches? I am especially interested in your practice of preservation with regard to plants. How do you deal with the (productive) contradiction of preserving something that keeps changing—the plant that, according to Goethe, for instance, is defined by its constant metamorphosis? Working with plants, are you exploring the very limits of the desire* *to congeal, freeze, maintain something the same, or preserve? If so, then how does growth, as a disruptive force, enter the fray of such a project?*

Heidi Norton: I am deeply interested in plants, and gaining a better understanding of them and sharing that with the viewer. But ultimately the plants are analogues to larger concepts of ecology, life, growth, change and death. Highlighting or displaying their mutability makes it palpable for the viewer. It is a slow, beautiful death that twists and turns in unpredictable directions. These works become representational samples of the physical laws of ecology. As Hans Haacke wrote in 1968: "A 'sculpture' that physically reacts to its environment is no longer to be regarded as an object. The range of outside factors affecting it, as well as its own radius of action, reach beyond the space it materially occupies. It thus merges with the environment in a relationship that is better understood as a 'system' of interdependent processes. These processes evolve without the viewer's empathy. He becomes a witness. A system is not imagined, it is real."[71]

Regarding the second question: When we preserve things, we arrest growth and age. In the case of the latex plant, the toxicity of the material in contact with the plant material caused those parts of the plant to die. Perhaps the new sprout was fed from anabolic energies produced by the dead parts. The growth is not disrupting the preservation but instead is highlighting it, accentuating it. Part of the metamorphosis of the plant is the entropic processes at work during the evolution of the plant. The ultimate preservation of life is something that is never attainable. These are futile bids to preserve time. The introduction of the resin, latex paint, or wax material to the plant marks a moment in which the plant is displaced; toxic material meets with the natural, paralyzing and interrupting growth. That moment of arrest occurs in a fraction of a second. This is similar to pushing the button of the shutter and capturing a fraction of time. There the plant

71. Hans Haacke, Statement for the exhibition catalog (New York: Howard Wise Gallery, January 1968).

156

is frozen in a state, escaping time. With the sculptures, the material attempts to stop time, and therefore growth. Regeneration may occur but death is inevitable.

(*to Marder*) *What is the difference between concepts of nature and ecology for you, and where does the plant fit into these places? What is a utopia according to a plant?*

Michael Marder: It's curious that we say *nature* and *ecology* in two different languages, even though both words are, of course, in English. Nature is derived from the Latin *natura* which, essentially, means "birth." The Greek word—*phusis*—that it translates is richer than that. *Phusis* is everything that springs up into existence, the total movement of growth, in which plants, animals, humans, and perhaps even mineral formations participate after their own fashion. What is at stake both in *phusis* and in *natura* is the question of beginnings, of origination, and a relation to the origin. As for *ecology*, here we have two words combined into one, again going back to Greek. *Eco-logy* refers to the *logos* of the *oikos*, or the inner articulation (you could say, the inherent reason or "logic") of the dwelling place. In this case, the stress shifts from the question of origins to that of how things work, how they develop in themselves and especially in relation to others. When we let our dwelling place, the environment, take care of itself, how does it organize itself? Since living beings are finite, so is their growth, which, at a certain point, gives place to decay, or, as often happens in the vegetal world, coexists with decay in the same plant (a branch of a tree can be decaying while the rest is thriving; the fallen leaves and fruits decay around the trunk, providing the roots with further mineral nourishment, and so on).

"What is a utopia according to a plant?" This is a very difficult question, and I will not pretend that I can give a satisfactory response to it, least of all "according to a plant." All I can do is offer a very preliminary reflection.

At first blush, utopia and vegetal life are absolutely incompatible. Plants are living beings rooted in the earth; utopia is a kind of non-existent place, a non-place. So, we seem to dream up our utopias in moments when we are least plant-like, that is, least attached to the places where we live or between which we live. At the same time, my philosophy of vegetal life has been sometimes accused of containing utopian elements, such as the peaceful coexistence of different forms of growth, for instance. This idea is utopian only if we continue to deny the vegetal heritage of our existence and adopt a purely animalistic notion of human nature as oppositional, where *homo homini lupus* (man is a wolf to man) and where we find ourselves in a "dog eat dog" world. As for the plants themselves, I think that their utopian moment is that of throwing their seeds or pollen to the wind or to the wings of insects. They entrust their future to chance, moving their potential offspring (more crudely put, their "genetic material") elsewhere, beyond the place of their growth from which they do not otherwise dislocate themselves. Perhaps, plants dream up their elsewhere in this throw of the dice. But here I must stop because it is impossible to speculate any further on this theme, without disrespecting the way the world appears (or doesn't appear) solely from their own living perspective.

29. On ethics (with Joe Humphreys)

1. You say a plant is an intelligent, social, complex being. What do you base this on?

The first thing we ought to remember is that plants are living beings, and it is a shame that this simple fact is still (or already) not self-evident today. Instead, in our agricultural practices, as much as in the prevailing conceptions of plants, we treat them as though they were organic machines for producing food, lumber, fuel, and so forth. The situation is very inauspicious, from the ethical point of view, but it holds out an unexpected promise for philosophers, who are quite fond of questioning those presuppositions that silently underpin a "commonsensical" approach to the world.

So, if plants are living beings, then they must be able to interact with the milieu where they grow (including other plants and insects) in order to obtain nourishment and tackle threatening situations. Otherwise, they would not have survived even for a week, let alone for hundreds of millions of years! Their interactions are also bound to be complex because environmental conditions change constantly, requiring an adequate response, a smart adjustment, from one moment to the next.

More than that, since they span diverse environments, from the underground world of minerals and moisture to the aboveground domain that we share with them, plants must be able to keep track of and adjust to countless factors at the same time–from the amount of sunlight to the presence of other plants' roots in the vicinity. And, indeed, they do! Contemporary plant sciences study, precisely, the different means by which plants can detect what is going on around them, how they respond accordingly and share this knowledge.

For instance, they can delay or accelerate their own flowering based on the information they have received from their neighbors through chemical cues emitted by the roots. If, in lab conditions, one plant is exposed to longer hours of light, not only will it blossom faster, but it will also transmit through the roots the news about these favorable circumstances to another plant that does not directly enjoy them. As a result, the recipient of this information will also blossom sooner than expected.[72]

I could amass many more examples such as this, but the point is not merely to regurgitate scientific findings. Rather, I want to liberate the notion of intelligence from its strict connection to the brain, central nervous system, or even animal sentience. I think that plants allow us to do just that—that is, they allow us to reconsider what we mean by intelligence in the absence of easily identifiable anatomical or physiological structures we tend to associate with the term and to imagine, more broadly, something like "the intelligence of life."

2. But there is no scientific evidence to show that plants are sentient beings. Is sentience a requirement for rights?

I wouldn't be so sure that there is no such evidence. Elsewhere, I have given the example of ethylene, "a classical plant hormone, is one such powerful anesthetic. This hormone, which relieves pain, is released in mechanically stressed plant tissues immediately after wounding."[73] Also, if you damage a leaf of a tomato or a tobacco plant, biochemical signals are sent from the site of injury to other parts, warning the rest of the plant about an attack (abiotic stress).[74]

It turns out that there are different kinds of sensitivity to threat, which sounds the alarm for a threatened living being. In humans and in many animals, pain plays the role of such a forewarning; in plants, distress is expressed in hormonal

---

72. Omer Falik, et al. "Say It with Flowers: Flowering Acceleration Through Root Communication." *Plant Signaling & Behavior*, 9(3), e28258.

73. Cf. Chapter 15 in the present book.

74. Chizuru Sato, et al. "Distal Transport of Exogenously Applied Jasmonoyl-Isoleucine with Wounding Stress", *Plant & Cell Physiology* 52(3), pp. 509-17.

and other sort of changes that fulfill the same function as pain. Conceptually, we would make the same mistake if we identified pain with sentience as the one where we equated human consciousness with intelligence. Just as there is no life without a minimum of intelligent response to the environment, there is no vitality without sentience that can and does assume all kinds shapes and forms.

What this implies for ethics is that "sentience as a requirement for rights" is too loose a prerequisite. As an alternative, we should develop more nuanced approaches, accounting for living beings that, albeit not resembling ourselves, pursue their own interests and ends.

3. You suggest (if I'm not oversimplifying it) that the key moral criterion is to be "respectful" of plants and their interests. Is it OK to eat plants if you are so respectful?

With regard to eating plants, it is helpful to know that we can nourish ourselves on some of their parts, such as fruits, without killing the entire organism. In non-Western cultures, this was actually an important criterion for an acceptable diet: Jainism prohibits the consumption of root vegetables, such as carrots or beets, since those parts are believed to house the souls of plants. Westerners can certainly learn a lot about respectful eating from these sources.

Having said that, I think that we put too much emphasis on personal choices in dietary and similar daily practices, while overlooking the fateful decisions on the part of transnational corporations that largely determine what we eat. The corporate commodification of agriculture is particularly disrespectful, in that it sacrifices, among other things, the potentialities of plants and their genetic integrity for the sake of higher profits.

Dietary choices certainly matter, and it would be wonderful if people were to make good decisions that would not be so totally destructive towards animals, plants, and the environment as they are today. But the ethics of individual responsibility is highly overrated in our societies, where respectful diets form small and extremely expensive pockets of resistance to the prevailing agricultural atrocities. There will be no justice or respect toward either plants or animals until agriculture and the economy as a whole are reorganized along non-capitalist lines.

4. Does your logic extend to meat-eating? Is it the disrespecting of animals, rather than their sentience, which makes it wrong to eat them?

Imagine that an animal is killed after having been artificially anaesthetized, that is, not experiencing any pain whatsoever. Does such a way of killing it make meat-eating acceptable, having effectively dealt with the problem of sentience? You see, that is why sentience as a criterion is insufficient and the notion of respect is inevitable in any postulation of an ethical diet.

5. It is OK to bulldoze a forest to make way for a children's hospital?

I am sure that there is plenty of space outside a forest for a children's hospital and that such medical facilities are more needed in populated areas. Many of our so-called moral choices are false not in the sense that we select a wrong option out of the two, but in the sense that they are formulated in terms that are misguided. Plants *or* animals, a forest *or* a hospital, and so forth are deceptive *either/or* choices. Which is why we need a more robust ethics than the one where we go through complex calculations of costs and benefits without reflecting about the pre-given parameters for decision-making.

6. What can humans learn from plants?

I have devoted many pages of my books and articles to the idea of learning from plants. If I were to sum up the most vital lesson plants have to teach us in one line, however, it would be: To grow not *against* but *together with* the environment, including other human beings, animals, and plants!

7. What's the most ethical dish one can eat?

Eating is not a very ethical activity in and of itself, because, in the process, the eater destroys the independent form of whatever is eaten and literally incorporates its materiality into her- or himself. The closest we come to eating ethically is by nourishing ourselves on locally grown fruit or vegetables. As I suggested elsewhere, though, a more significant question is *how* one eats, rather than *what*. Does one admit and show respect to the other potentialities of one's sources of nutrition, resisting the urge to convert them entirely into food? Does one let a being that provides one with sustenance live? Does one give thanks for this gift of nourishment?

30. On politics (with Margarida Mendes)[75]

1. Your essay "Vegetal Democracy: The Plant that is not One"[76] departs from an analysis of plant growth schematics, while reflecting on political structures. What can we learn from thinking politics through the observation of non-human entities?

Human patterns of collective organization cannot break entirely with similar configurations in the physical, natural world. To think otherwise is to idealize politics entirely, reducing it to the activity of disembodied spirit. Indeed, traditionally, humans turned to animals as a reference point and recognized in their own societies certain unmistakable features of animal groupings, for instance, of ants or bees. Aristotle famously defined the human as a "political animal," *zoōn politikon.*

My question, in turn, is: "What if we think about ourselves as political plants?" The main difference between plants and animals is that the former are not organismic units, that is to say, self-enclosed living totalities where each part is subordinated to the demands of a coherent whole. So, if we want to escape from proto-fascism in our political thought, whereby the state is equated to an organic whole and individuals to its mostly insignificant organs, we must seek a vegetal model of the political. The outcome of this exercise is going to be a sort of anarchic proliferation of multiplicities, of branches and twigs that retain their semi-independence while participating in the overall growth of plant-society. Such bio-politics would be incompatible with the spirit of sacrifice, logically expected within the limits of an organismic arrangement; instead, it would encourage the growing of all within a

---

75. A version of this interview was published in Katarina Chuchalina & Vladislav Shapovalov (eds.), *Urban Fauna Lab: Valley of Beggars* (Moscow: V-A-C & Marsilio, 2015).

76. Michael Marder, "Vegetal Democracy: The Plant that is not One." In Artemy Magun (ed.), *Politics of the One: On Unity and Multiplicity in Contemporary Thought* (London & New York: Bloomsbury, 2012), pp. 115-130.

mutually supportive environment, where there isn't a con-flict—nor even a clear-cut division—between the individual and the collective. That, for me, is a critically important po-litical lesson of plants.

2. There has been a recent inquiry in Utrecht into the takeover of its underground paths and canals by a fern plague. A study group was gathered to map and analyse all the fern species present there, from which a particular species, Azolla filiculoides, has been identified. An indisputable image of the parasite emerges here. What are your thoughts about the entropic growth of green structures that exist in parallel with anthropogenic ones?

I am not so sure that vegetal "entropic" growth unfolds side-by-side with the propagation of anthropogenic structures. Our growth is not as orderly as we think and it is certainly subject to entropy, like everything in the material world. Nor are human processes and categories entirely separate from other modes of life, no matter how much we try to suppress and repress these nonhuman manifestations of vitality in us. Much of the human biomass is comprised on bacteria, many of them beneficial for the functioning of the digestive and other bodily systems. The human neo-cortex coevolved with the microorganisms that cover it and that probably played an important role in the development of our intelligence. Rath-er than a small island in the sea of organic life and an even larger ocean of the inorganic universe, the human is a point of intersection for diverse types of existence, not to mention the classical elements of water, fire, earth, and air. In effect, much of the current environmental crisis is due to our refusal to come to terms with our co-imbrication with the rest of the world, which we unabashedly shape in our own image, heavily skewed toward abstract intelligence. It is only from this vantage point that the entropy of "raw" nature seems to be opposed to well-structured, logically explicable anthropo-genic processes.

As for parasitism, again, I have my doubts that it makes sense to draw a solid demarcation line between "the host" and "the

166

parasites." What we deem to be hosts are themselves, necessarily, parasitic on a larger milieu they inhabit; the humans, seen from a certain perspective, are the parasites of the earth. After all, etymologically, parasitism refers to networks of nourishment, whereby a living entity feeds alongside (*para*) some other entity or entities. So, while certain microorganisms nourish themselves on our bodies, we nourish ourselves on the earth–hence, on whatever issues from it.

In the case of plants, the phenomenon of parasitism is more interesting still. We will not be amiss if we conclude that each part of a plant is parasitic on other parts, even as this composite growing being is parasitic on the soil wherein it is rooted. You will recall that it is impossible to definitively establish the boundaries of vegetal individuals. On the one hand, a twig, detached from the mother-plant, can develop its own roots, if provided with enough moisture and mineral nutrients. On the other hand, ostensibly separate plants, including trees, may share their system of roots and, therefore, formally belong to the same mega-plant as its outgrowths. Who is the parasite and who is the host here? All I can say is that plants grow on, live on, and nourish themselves on other plants… *ad infinitum*. This happens within the "same" plant that combines a multiplicity of potentially independent plants, traversed by a common network of nourishment. And it also happens between "different" plants, such as moss growing on tree trunks or grafts of a peach on a pear tree. We tend to classify this latter situation as parasitic. But the way any given plant or a community of plants belonging to the same species is structured is not really qualitatively distinct from such an arrangement.

3. Plants grow exponentially as modular unities that spread through the ground as perfect rhizomes. They remind me of cybernetic systems. How do you see the comparison, if any, between the behavioral growth of plants and computational processes?

You are right to observe that, far from one type of plant roots, the rhizome is the synecdoche of vegetal growth in general.

Lacking a single command center that could orchestrate all of its development, a plant grows by iterations, replicating already existing structures. It branches out above and below ground, creating baroque-like gardens upon gardens upon gardens, as Leibniz once put it.

It is quite enticing to envision this kind of growth as an open network and, subsequently, to re-project the computational grid back onto plants. Not surprisingly, today, the network is our preferred master-concept, an imaginary key to the understanding of the environment, of society, of bodily functions, and of thinking itself. But I, myself, would not rush to this conclusion. Why?

First, we must historicize our conceptual practices, an endeavor which will allow us to understand that the image of the network says much more about us, who overuse it, than about the phenomena it is meant to explain. This image has merely replaced the early modern metaphor of a machine, admittedly less flexible than a network but similarly overarching as an explanatory device.

Second, we should accept that there isn't one master-concept, useful for elucidating everything in the world. Even if the time of great metaphysical narratives is apparently over, science, or better, scientificity, carries on the legacy of metaphysics in the name of a non- or even an anti-metaphysical worldview. To qualify as a metaphysician, you do not need to relate everything either to God or to a God-like construct; you only need to believe that a single foundation undergirds all reality, the latter being epiphenomenal in reference to this foundation. Cybernetics and the network-theory of society, nature, and intelligence are the cornerstones of the contemporary metaphysics that refuses to go under this name.

Third, we ought to revive the question of life, which remains conceptually elusive and irreducible to computation of the best course of action at a given conjuncture between an organism and its environment. The provocation I would

168

like to throw to the readers is to think life not as another all-encompassing metaphysical concept, but as an inherently meaningful framework—better yet, a multiplicity of frameworks—interpretable "from within" in the practices of living by microorganisms, plants, animals, humans…

Having said that, I must admit that many of my colleagues in plant sciences and philosophy alike favor a computational theory of plant intelligence. They study, for instance, flowering decisions of cherry trees based on the comparisons of day length, carried out by these plants with the help of their cellular memories of the last sunrays, gathered over a specific stretch of time. I do not want to deny the value of these studies nor to doubt their contribution to shaping the concept of plant intelligence. What I take issue with is the idea that these and similar computations exhaust the content and, especially, the form of intelligence. Just as a human being whose thinking is defined exclusively in terms of calculation would be impoverished and robot-like at best, a plant that "thinks" and lives along these lines alone would be something like a green, mean, computing machine.

4. The notion of deterritorialisation is intrinsic to the history of vegetable life, not only due to the aerial migration of seeds, but also by their colonial exploitation. In your forthcoming book co-written with Luce Irigaray you write about your personal relation to vegetable life as a mode of thinking exile and uprooting. Discontinuity and manipulation are evident characteristics in terms of how humans regulate and make use of natural entities, addressed by them as subjectless mass. How do you relate to the position of the subaltern here?

It is true that, despite popular beliefs, plants are very mobile. Not only do their seeds and pollen migrate far and wide, but they also move within their milieu in ways that are different from locomotion. Their decay, growth, and metamorphosis constitute three other types of movement, which Aristotle recognized in his *Physics*. Still, plants represent, for us, the archetype of a firm attachment to a place, of which we are increasingly nostalgic in the age of globalization.

Ethical problems arise when we associate embeddedness in a locale with passivity. In this instance, plants appear to be the nonhuman incarnations of feudal surfs, completely enchained to the context of their growth. The praise of dislocation and uprooting is the flip side of the same coin that links mobility to active subjectivity, and anchoring in a place–to the passive existence of a "subjectless mass," as you aptly put it. In an effort to prevent such a violent schematization of different life-forms, we cannot bypass the ancient Greeks, who thought of life as the capacity for self-movement and self-organization. As we have just established, together with Aristotle, plants are capable of moving in every one of the four ways he pinpointed. So, it follows that they cannot be justifiably treated as dumb "matter primed for reproduction," in the words of Kant.

What I cannot accept from the Greeks, however, is the ontological hierarchy, in which they lined up all living beings. Restoring to plants their self-moving, self-organizing traits is not enough if their subjectivity remains inferior to those of animals and humans. As an alternative, I propose that we strain to imagine, at the limits of our theoretical imagination, how plants construct a world for themselves; how they produce the structures of embodied sense, meaningful for them; what they pay attention to; where they locate the foci of significance; and how they act and are acted upon by the world that is imbued with meaning *for them*. The preliminary name I have given to this project is *phyto-phenomenology*, or the phenomenology of vegetal life. I do not know whether an endeavor like this can really come to fruition, but, at least, it is worth giving it a try.

31. On plant-thinking
(with Ilda Teresa Castro)

1. Recent years have seen a great production (of your books, book chapters and articles) concerning plants. What motivates your interest in that subject?

When I started working on the "philosophy of vegetal life" in 2008, there were virtually no studies on the topic. When I mentioned to friends and acquaintances that I was working with plants and philosophy, they usually had a puzzled look on their faces but, invariably, wanted to know more about such an bizarre combination.

Initially, I was simply dissatisfied with the fashionable investigations of "the question of the animal" in the humanities. The animals that were usually studied in that context were highly individuated ones: either similar to humans (other primates, chimpanzees…) or those we are used to think of as pets (dogs and cats) or, in the best of cases, other species we consider benevolent and intelligent based on our own measures of these criteria (dolphins, elephants, etc.). "Interspecies ethics" did not really account for hyenas, mosquitoes, or any variety of plants, as it strove to create a larger-than-human community of living beings.

As I attempted to make a modest contribution toward filling this lacuna, it quickly became obvious that a single book would not suffice. For instance, the ethical and political issues surrounding plant life have to be addressed in a separate monograph, which is still in the works. You can, nonetheless, see the outlines of such a study in the book chapters and articles I published over the last few years.

Despite all the research already done, the field of the philosophy of plant life remains, quite literally, fertile. We have yet to delve into the aesthetics of plants, informed by the emergent theoretical approaches, and we have barely scratched the surface when it comes to the importance of vegetal processes in our own thinking.

2. What are the main purposes, similarities and differences between Plant-Thinking: A Philosophy of Vegetal Life (*Columbia UP, 2013*), The Philosopher's Plant: An Intellectual Herbarium (*Columbia UP, 2014*), *and the forthcoming book (with Luce Irigaray),* Through Vegetal Being *(Columbia UP, 2016)?*

Plant-Thinking wished to clear the ground for a reconceptualization of the place of plants in the history of Western philosophy and to reconfigure an ontology of vegetal life that would give vegetal temporality, freedom, and mode of relating to the world their due. It was a book written primarily for philosophers, interested in extending their preoccupations with animals to other non-human and non-animal forms of life.

In turn, *The Philosopher's Plant* was conceived as an introduction to philosophy for those interested in the discipline, as well as, for those already well versed in it, an alternative itinerary through intellectual history extending from Plato to our days. In this book, I zero in on biographical episodes in the lives of twelve prominent philosophers that, in one way or another, feature plants, with which each of them is associated. I then explain their basic ideas and systems of thought with the help of vegetal examples, images, and metaphors. Finally, I discuss the contributions made (and obstacles posed) by these philosophers to our understanding of plants and to the budding philosophy of vegetal life.

I did everything I could to make the book both light and intriguing. It was a pleasure to compose also because it gave me a chance to collaborate with a French artist, Mathilde Roussel, who turned it into a true "herbarium" thanks to her beautiful paintings that open each chapter. In general, I hope that *The Philosopher's Plant* will draw people to philosophy, as much as create a set of connections between ideas and actual plant specimens I discuss in it (from wheat to water lily; pears to palm trees…)

As for the *Through Vegetal Being*, a manuscript I've just finished writing with Luce Irigaray, this book is perhaps even more unconventional. In it, we mix fragments of our own biographies with stories and reflections about plants. We think of this book as an encounter between us "through" the mediation of plants—one that offers a more complete approach to vegetal life thanks to the framework of sexuate difference, within which our text unfolds and which keeps our perspectives separate while interrelating them.

32. Debate on plant and animal ethics (with Gary Francione)

1. How does plant ethics relate to veganism?

Michael Marder: Plant ethics shares with veganism a strong commitment to justice, which is to say, to the reduction of violence humans perpetrate against other living beings. It is by no means a threat to or an invalidation of veganism. Rather, plant ethics is an open invitation to fine-tune our dietary practices in keeping with the philosophical and scientific insights into what plants are, what they are capable of, and what our relation to them should be.

Jean-Jacques Rousseau made a useful distinction between perfection and perfectibility, arguing that the latter defines human beings. If veganism thinks of its moral bases as perfectible, it will, I believe, admit plant ethics into its midst. Doubts sometimes arise as to whether or not veganism is a genuinely philosophical position when its unbending commitment is mistaken for doctrinaire rigidity, and its morality—for self-righteous moralizing. A serious engagement with plant ethics will finally dispel all such suspicions, as it will demonstrate a dynamic thinking behind veganism, ready to push its own limits.

This does not mean that, having entertained the real possibility of violence against plants, vegans would throw their hands up in despair and concede that it is pointless to alleviate animal suffering by refusing to consume animal flesh and by-products. What it implies is that they would not rest on the laurels of their accomplishments but would take into account the residual violence against other living beings, such as plants, thoroughly instrumentalized by the same logic that underpins human domination over other animal species.

Gary Francione: If plants are not sentient—if they have no subjective awareness—then they have no interests. That is, they cannot desire, or want, or prefer anything. There is simply no reason to believe that plants have *any* level of perceptual awareness or *any* sort of mind that prefers, wants, or desires anything.

Although I am in many respects sympathetic to Jain ethics, and in particular to the notion that we should never engage in intentional violence against sentient beings, I do not share the Jain notion that plants and microscopic organisms, because they are alive, have souls. You really need that sort of approach to start to make sense of your position.

I do believe that we have an obligation not to eat more plants than we need to live, but that is because I think that overeating is a form of violence to our own bodies. I also believe that we have an obligation to all sentient inhabitants of the planet not to use more non-sentient resources than we need.

In both cases, we have obligations that concern plants but these obligations are not owed directly to plants.

I am all in favor of vegans perfecting their moral bases and I urge all vegans to consider embracing a progressive understanding of human rights that rejects racism, sexism, homophobia, classism, ageism, and all other forms of discrimination, which are indistinguishable from speciesism.

Michael Marder: As I have pointed out, contemporary research in plant sciences gives us ample reasons to believe that plants are aware of their environment—for instance, thanks to the roots that are capable of altering their growth pattern in moving toward resource-rich soil or away from nearby roots of other members of the same species. To ignore such evidence in favor of a stereotypical view of plants as thing-like is counterproductive, both for ethics and for our understanding of what or who they are.

When we, humans, use ourselves as a measuring stick against which everything clsc in world is evaluated, then an anthropomorphic image of sentience and intelligence comes to govern our ethics. True: the life of plants resembles our living patterns to a lesser extent than the life of animals. But to use this as a cornerstone of ethics and a justification for rejecting the moral claim plants have on us is a case of extreme speciesism.

Gary Francione: Speciesism occurs when the interests of a being are accorded less or no weight solely on the basis of species. To say that a being has interests is to say that the being has some sort of mind—*any* sort of mind—that prefers, desires, or wants. It is to say that there is some*one* who prefers, desires, or wants. You cannot act with speciesism with respect to a being that has no interests, such as a plant.

Your entire argument rests on your confusing a *reaction* with a *response*. If you put an electrical current through a wire that is attached to a bell, the bell will ring. The bell reacts; it does not respond. It is as absurd to say that a bell has a "nonconscious response" as it is to say that a plant does.

What would it mean for ethical eating if plants were shown to suffer pain and have feelings, even intentionality?

Michael Marder: We run the risk of caricaturizing plant intelligence studies when we directly translate animal and human sensoria into the sentience of plants (such as tomatoes) that, when attacked by insects, biochemically signal the danger to other specimens nearby and render their leaves unpalatable. It is, however, more productive to keep in mind what in *Plant-Thinking* I termed "the nonconscious intentionality" of plants—their extended and dispersed striving, expressed in growth and reproduction. What is the moral claim of this intentionality upon us?

Ancient Greeks thought that every living being tends toward the Good, in each case appropriate to its kind of existence.

It is clear that, although they might not cognitively know it, plants are and act in ways consistent with what is good for them. We must at the very least take this "vegetal good" into account in our ethical treatment of plants.

At the same time, their intentionality cannot be easily integrated into a coherent unity or a totality we usually associate with an organism. Plants are remarkable in how they may shed almost any part and still germinate from whatever remains in the loose assemblage that they are. The dispersion of vegetal intentionality shifts the moral focus onto communities of plants that disrupt all our anthropocentric distinctions between the individual and the collective.

At the risk of oversimplification, I would suggest that ethical eating demands that we respect plant communities, paying attention both to the methods of their cultivation and to their reproductive possibilities.

Gary Francione: To answer the question, if plants were able to suffer, or had intentionality, we would be under an obligation to accord plant interests moral consideration. I have not yet seen your book but I suspect that, at best, you have provided more information about the reactions of plants. But no one would deny that plants react to stimuli. There is, however, not one shred of evidence about which I am aware that plants suffer or have any intentional states.

Let me say that even if, contrary to all that we know, plants are sentient, how would that change our moral behavior? It takes many pounds of plant protein to produce one pound of flesh. Assuming that we concluded we were not obligated to commit suicide, we would still be morally obligated to consume plants rather than consume flesh or animal products that required more plants than if we consumed those plants directly, and that also involved animal deaths.

As a general matter, you appear to be confusing being alive and having reactions to stimuli with having responses that require moral consideration. You are arguing that every life form has a "nonconscious intentionality" that requires our moral consideration. So, in addition to plants, we would have to consider moral obligations to bacteria. After all, they are alive. They have "nonconscious intentionality." Every time we wash our faces, or brush our teeth, we are engaging in violence because we "instrumentalize" bacteria. We need to respect communities of bacteria.

Do you really believe that?

Michael Marder: You presuppose that plant reactions are automatic and quasi-mechanical, as opposed to the freedom of animal and human responses. But, just as humans and animals often act on reflex, plants engage in nonconscious determinations of the course of their growth, above and below the ground.

You ask where to draw the line of moral considerability. We should certainly not reject the possibility of respecting communities of bacteria without analyzing the issue seriously. But my research has to do with the life of plants, not bacteria. It is counterproductive to recreate hierarchies of beings, instead of giving each kind of being its due.

Gary Francione: Again, you are confusing reaction or reflex with a response and your framework would *necessarily* apply to bacteria and *anything* alive that reacts in any way. There is no way to distinguish among beings, all of whom have what you call "nonconscious determination." And to the extent that you exclude the bell from the moral community, you create a hierarchy among things that react.

What, at bottom, is the nature of the dispute between us?

Michael Marder: It is still somewhat early to offer exhaustive commentary on the nature of the dispute between us. I will limit myself to three basic points.

First, it seems that the "food chain," at the top of which we, humans, presumably are, is the contemporary reflection of the metaphysical Great Chain of Being. In my view it is not enough to meddle with only one aspect of this structure (the relation between humans and animals), while leaving the rest intact. I would think that we need to undermine such hierarchical formations in all respects, and I have yet to hear my vegan friends endorse this position.

Second, Western philosophers have thought about plants at best as deficient animals, and therefore the violence against animals was magnified manifold when it came to plants. If vegans subscribe to this position, they appear still to be operating in the spirit of the very philosophical tradition that has devalued animal lives.

Last but not least is the question of strategy and of principles. It does not make sense to me to advocate something clearly unethical—a total instrumentalization of certain living beings, such as plants—in the name of ethics—a complete de-instrumentalization of other kinds of living beings, such as animals. In such advocacy, the end does not justify the means; rather, the means annul the end.

Gary Francione: It may be too early to offer an "exhaustive commentary" about our dispute but I think a simple commentary is in order: *I reject completely the notion that we can have direct moral obligations to plants. I reject completely that plants have any interests whatsoever.*

You disagree. What else is there to say?

In my own work on animal ethics, I have rejected anthropocentrism completely in maintaining that all sentient beings are equal for the purpose of having the moral right not to be treated exclusively as a human resource. But to say that by drawing a line between the sentient and the non-sentient, I am invoking the Great Chain of Being or operating "in the spirit of the very philosophical tradition that devalued animal lives," assumes that there is some*one* here to devalue. There isn't.

I should note in the 30 years I have been doing this work, when I discuss this issue with people who are not vegans, the conversation almost invariably turns to a sudden solicitude for the "interests" of the vegetables on our plates.

We both know that the primary audience for your book will not be vegans who want to ponder whether they are under-inclusive ethically, but those who claim that we should skip over the interests of the cow and worry about whether the carrot had a tough harvesting season.

Please do not misunderstand me; I am not saying that a scholar should not pursue a topic because his or her theory or work may be used in a particular way. I am, however, saying that in a world in which we kill 56 billion sentient beings a year for food (not counting fish), the idea that we need to think about plants or risk being accused of "self-righteous moralizing" is, on many levels, disturbing.

Michael Marder: Before deciding whether or not we have any obligations toward plants, it is vital to ask what (or who) they are, instead of acting upon a preconceived notion. This question is at the core of my book. Any non-dogmatic acceptance or rejection of the moral considerability of plants must rely on sound ontological foundations.

Gary Francione: I am at the disadvantage of not having yet read your book but you acknowledge that plants are not sentient. In my view, that is all the "ontological foundation" that is needed.

I assume that you are vegan, or, at least, that you see veganism as a baseline requirement of justice toward sentient animals. If, as you say, plant ethics involves a commitment to justice just as veganism does, and that the former does not undermine the latter, you would, it seems be committed to veganism as a non-controversial position, even if you think it remains perfectible. If, however, this enterprise is really about putting cows and corn in the same group, then it would most certainly be an attempt to undermine veganism.

Thank you for this most interesting exchange.

Univocal Publishing
411 N. Washington Ave, Suite 10
Minneapolis, MN 55401
www.univocalpublishing.com

ISBN 9781937561673

Jason Wagner, Drew S. Burk
(Editors)
All materials were printed and bound
in May 2016 at Univocal's atelier
in Minneapolis, USA.

This work was composed in Garamond.
The paper is Hammermill 98.
The letterpress cover was printed
on Crane's Lettra Fluorescent.
Both are archival quality and acid-free.